A Song to My City

WASHINGTON
DC

A Song to My City
WASHINGTON
DC

CAROL LANCASTER

WITH DOUGLAS FARRAR

Georgetown University Press / Washington, DC

Library of Congress Cataloging-in-Publication

Names: Lancaster, Carol, author. | Farrar, Doug, author
Title: A song to my city : Washington, DC / Carol Lancaster with
    Doug Farrar.
Description: Washington, DC : Georgetown University Press, 2016. |
    Includes bibliographical references and index.
Identifiers: LCCN 2016024171 (print) | LCCN 2016040474 (ebook) |
    ISBN 9781626163836 (hc : alk. paper) | ISBN 9781626163843 (eb) |
    ISBN 9781626163843 ()
Subjects: LCSH: Washington (D.C.)—History. | Washington (D.C.)—
    Biography. | L'Enfant, Pierre Charles, 1754-1825. | Shepherd,
    Alexander Robey, 1835–1902. | Barry, Marion, 1936–2014.
Classification: LCC F194 .L34 2016 (print) | LCC F194 (ebook) | DDC
    975.3—dc23
LC record available at https://lccn.loc.gov/2016024171

∞ This book is printed on acid-free paper meeting the requirements
of the American National Standard for Permanence in Paper for
Printed Library Materials.

17 16   9 8 7 6 5 4 3 2   First printing

Printed in the United States of America

Jacket design by Tim Green, Faceout Studio.
DC Row Houses by Roberson Photos, courtesy of Getty Images.
Twilight in the swamps of Roosevelt Island by Cameron Whitman,
courtesy of Stocksy.
Text design by Coghill Composition Company.

Contents

Foreword

CAROL LANCASTER, my mother, died of a brain tumor on October 22, 2014, in Washington, DC. In her professional life, which was dedicated to scholarly work and government service, her writings were mostly articles, books, and academic papers, with the books being policy-oriented explorations of various aspects of foreign assistance. This book is unique, the only one Carol wrote out of love alone. It was her most cherished effort, created in the margins of her very busy professional and family life. It is a love letter to the city that she adored, the one in which she chose to live and work.

This book is the last one that my mother wrote. She finished a draft of the manuscript soon before she became ill. After her death I consulted with two of her friends and former colleagues at Georgetown—Maurice Jackson and Gail Griffith—to complete the manuscript. I owe them great thanks.

Many Washingtonians have come here from other places, drawn by the call of service or power or by a commitment to try to make a difference, and have adopted this city as their own. Others may live here their whole lives, just as their parents did, and work for the government—the single biggest employer—or in any number of sectors that support the city.

More often than not these Washingtonians, like residents of other big cities, go about their business and simply try to get by and get ahead.

These two groups of Washingtonians live and work side by side but barely know each other. Many living in "political" Washington only casually acknowledge the existence of the other community. Carol's perspective on this city is unique, because the arc of her life moved from one community to the other.

Carol lived out the intrinsically American rags to riches story and pulled herself up by the bootstraps. In her case, however, she moved from the working class to become a senior government official and the dean at one of the country's most prestigious academic institutions.

Carol was born poor and spent the early part of her life in a farmhouse in Anacostia, when such homes still existed. Her parents, Lelia and Henry Lancaster, only completed high school. During a period of white flight from the city, the Lancasters moved to Temple Hills, Maryland. There Carol lived a working-class life filled with many challenges. Their home was small, and the way they lived reflected their limited resources. Whenever I visited as a young boy, my granny would make me snacks of toast with butter and sugar, telling me that my mother ate that instead of candy because "it was cheaper that way." Growing up, when I wanted to watch television after I had finished my homework and eaten dinner, my mother would frequently tell me that her family had only had a TV for a few months, and when it broke there was no money to fix it. She was actually pleased it wasn't repaired because it meant she had more time to read.

Carol attended Oxon Hill High School, where she excelled, particularly in foreign language, and her guidance counselor urged her to consider attending Georgetown University to study language. Carol's parents didn't have enough money to cover both tuition and room and board, so she became a "day hop," traveling by bus each day from her parents' home to her classes at the university.

She was one of the first women to attend Georgetown's School of Foreign Service. She would later become dean of that school, but as a student, she was simply looking for a way out of her working-class life in Temple Hills. Her mother's life experiences had limited her own horizons, and though she believed in her daughter's abilities, she exhibited a fatalistic pessimism when it came to Carol's future potential.

When Carol graduated from Georgetown, her mother said, "Time to come home and join the typing pool." Carol informed her mother that, instead, she had accepted a Fulbright scholarship to study in La Paz, Bolivia.

When she departed for Bolivia, Carol left behind the Washington she had known. When she returned nearly a decade later, after completing her studies in Bolivia and receiving a master's degree and PhD in economics from the London School of Economics, she was similar to the other well-educated, determined professionals who arrive in the political stew of Washington each year, anxious to make their marks in the city. Her experience growing up as a member of the working class in Washington, though, did imbue her with an objective fairness and generosity that, all who knew her would attest, defined her friendships and professional demeanor. Above all, she sought to bring people together, deal with others on their merits, and do her best to help those in need.

She went on to work in Congress as a legislative aide; at the Office of Management and Budget, the State Department, and the US Agency for International Development (USAID); and for Georgetown University. Ultimately she became the first woman, and first alumna, to be named dean of the School of Foreign Service.

Carol was both proud of and wounded by her humble beginnings. Over the course of her life, she lost touch with much of her family. She joked with me that her relatives were either truckers or preachers. Although she did not maintain relationships with members of her extended family, nor they with her, she instilled in me a pride of my Washington roots. She often reminded me that I was a fourth-generation Washingtonian, whose ancestors had immigrated here with nothing, built lives, served in the military, and struggled to succeed in this city.

I feel fortunate to live with my wife in Washington, DC, and have my father nearby. My mother lived such a full life in this city. Wherever I go, I feel as though I am tracing her footsteps. When I stroll through Georgetown's campus, dine at a Dupont Circle bistro, go to a farmers' market, play for my men's league soccer teams at a local high school, visit an art gallery, or attend a meeting at one of Washington's many nonprofit think tanks or government buildings, I imagine her having preceded me in those locations. I go about my daily life and have chance recollections and remembrances—many happy memories—spring on me at unexpected moments. I am grateful she left this gift to me.

What follows is her final expression of love for the city where she was born, triumphed, and died. I hope that seeing Washington, DC, through her eyes, with her remarkable insights and appreciation for its history and people, gives readers a new perspective on the city she loved so much.

Douglas Farrar

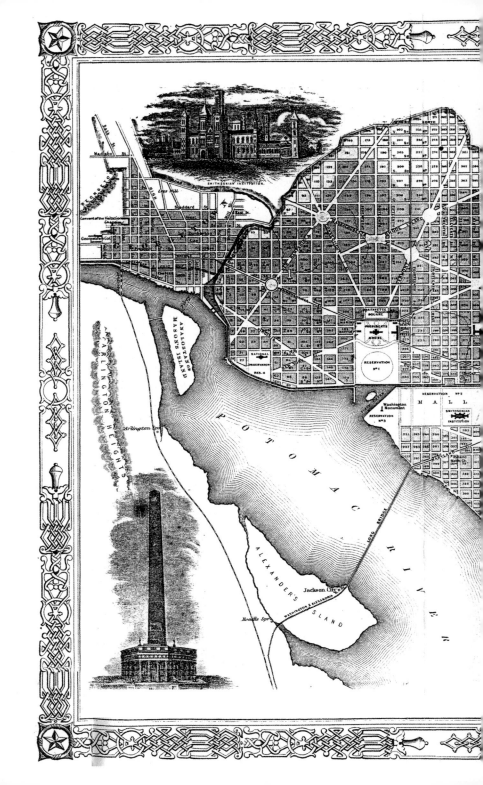

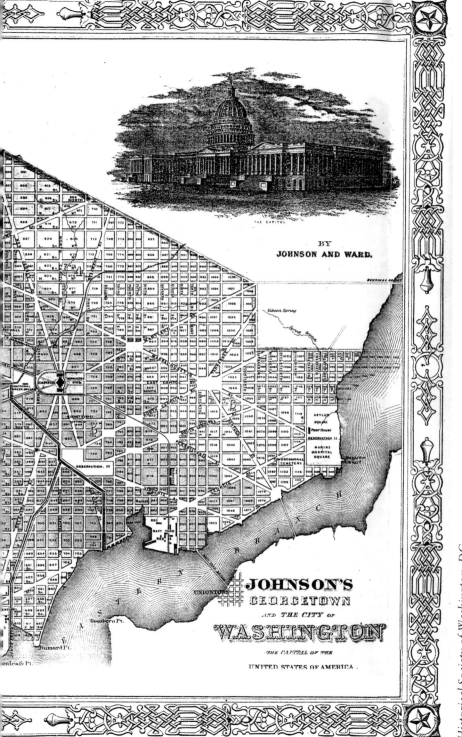

BY
JOHNSON AND WARD.

JOHNSON'S
GEORGETOWN
AND THE CITY OF
WASHINGTON
THE CAPITAL OF THE
UNITED STATES OF AMERICA.

myself asking these questions when visiting a new city. They are the questions *A Song to My City* tries to answer for Washington, DC.

So why write a book on Washington, DC? The capital of any country is of interest. In its memorials, architecture, and art, the capital usually celebrates the best a country has to offer. It is worthwhile getting to know the city of Washington for what it reflects about America. But there is so much more. Washington is different from most other American cities. It is a planned city in a country that for a long time disliked cities and abhorred government planning. That it survived remarkably true to its original plan is a miracle. As a result, it is a city of grand public spaces in a country that has paid little attention to such concerns in its reckless charge toward urban development. It is also a city that was long regarded as a cultural wasteland but has become a place of rich artistic diversity and perhaps among the most intellectually active places in the United States. It is an urban space whose downtown—decayed, burned out, and virtually abandoned in the aftermath of the 1968 riots—has developed into a venue for entertainment, with amenities and a vibrant street life. In short, the city is revitalizing rapidly with an uptick in its population, part of a broader trend evident in several other American cities and perhaps a sign that America's traditional preference for suburban space and cars is gradually beginning to turn more toward urban living.

Many Americans, identifying Washington solely with national politics, will still wonder, why bother to write a book about the city? While treasuring its symbols, they may regard Washington as a den of political iniquity, a place of opportunism, self-promotion, partisanship, and sleazy deal making. It is the place some politicians like to run against. Others view Washington as boring and bureaucratic. I often hear the remark, "There is no *there* there." Still others see it as a place of crime and corrupt politicians, as unsafe and unsavory. Why would anyone want to write about such a place?

Those images do not reflect the Washington of today. Of course, as the capital of a great nation, Washington naturally has politics at its core, and some of its political theater can be both amusing and repellent. For those who love politics, Washington is a paradise. For those who do not, Washington can be an exasperating place to live. However, sometimes, the latter types get bitten by the political bug and join the former types. They may even get what President Woodrow Wilson called "Potomac fever." Its most severe symptoms are said to be a delusion of grandeur, a loss of memory (i.e., who elected or appointed you, anyway?), and a deterioration in language (involving the frequent use of bureaucratic terms and acronyms known only inside the Washington Beltway). It leads us to look over the shoulder of the person we are with at a reception to see if someone else (more important) we should be talking to is present. It means with a new book, we turn first to the bibliography to see if we are cited there. Many in Washington suffer from this fever, it is true.

But behind all the political maneuvering is something sacred: It is the revolutionary idea, first tried in modern times in the United States of America, that people—however selfish and self-interested they naturally are—can somehow govern themselves in peace and prosperity. What is so often missed in the day-to-day politics of Washington is that the many conflicts and compromises turn on legitimate differences over the basic issues of democracy. Who should govern and how? Who should influence government, and how should government authority itself be limited? What rights should minorities have in a system of majority rule? What is the meaning of freedom and equality?

Much of the history of Washington and many of the famous buildings and statues in the city relate to individuals who have debated and sometimes fought and died to decide those basic questions. Thus, the pomp and circumstance of Washington that so many lament is ultimately all about our most treasured values—that is, our very identity. Indeed, to be an American is not to be a member of an ethnic group but to embrace the idea of political equality and of self-government. Washington, DC, from its establishment in 1800 until today is the manifestation—sometimes flawed, sometimes successful—of that ideal and the long struggle to realize it. The city's buildings, landscape, monuments, and the national politics at its core are all testimony of our great dream. In this profound sense, Washington is the most "American" of cities.

But Washington does not look like any other American city. It has a grand, monumental core framed by two rivers, the Anacostia and the Potomac. Seen from the air, the city center resembles a park with its large, green spaces and clusters of white buildings and familiar monuments. Its low skyline, its broad, radiating avenues, its parks, and its thousands of trees give a feeling of space and sky and highlight the presence of nature in a city of human proportions.

Washington is also a city for walking. Visitors and residents alike savor not only its great memorials and historical venues but also the very different neighborhoods of Georgetown, Capitol Hill, or Dupont Circle—places to wander, to look and stop for coffee or a drink, and to walk some more, letting curious or charming streets lead them along. In short, it is a setting for the flaneur. Edmund White tells us the almost untranslatable French word means "that aimless stroller who loses himself in the crowd, who has no destination and goes wherever caprice or curiosity directs his or her steps." Such people experience a city on foot. White, who strolled and wrote in Paris, also has warned that "Americans are particularly ill-suited to be *flâneurs*. . . . [T]hey are always driven by the urge towards self-improvement." But with all of its museums and historical sites scattered around town, Washington may in fact be just the place for a conscientious American flaneur.

Yet the city does have its problems. One in five of its citizens live in poverty, and almost all of the poor are black or Latino, the consequence in part of a long history of past discrimination. The population of the city is majority African American, and the middle class—both black and white—is large. But Washington in many ways remains economically and socially segregated in where people live and socialize. Race and social class are ever-present elements in local politics, in social relations, and, often, in the minds of Washingtonians.

The city government still suffers from years of mismanagement and from the fact that despite a degree of home rule, Washington, DC—unlike any other city in the United States—is ultimately controlled by Congress. Congress can reverse the city's laws, change its budgets, and disregard the will of its citizens, whose nonvoting delegate has only a limited voice in that body. The freeways, built in the city in the 1960s during a national paroxysm of highway construction, still disfigure parts of the city. The rapidly spreading revitalization and gentrification of Washington has pushed the poor out of the increasingly expensive downtown neighborhoods, underlining the need for low-income housing and public transportation. Homelessness is still evident in downtown parks and streets, and crime, while substantially less than in the recent past, remains a concern. Public schools in Washington remain among the worst in the nation though efforts to reform them have intensified. And Washington has one of the country's most trying commuting problems. Several hundred thousand people enter the city every day from its sprawling suburbs to work, and many of them travel by car, leading to legendary backups on major highways. How these problems are resolved will shape the Washington of the future.

Finally, to answer the question of why I should write a book about Washington, DC, I am a third-generation Washingtonian; there are not many of us. My mother's large family (ten children) moved to DC from the Shenandoah Valley in the early part of the twentieth century. They were part of a broad movement of Americans around that time who migrated from farms to cities as they searched for better lives.

After my grandfather died, the family lived hard lives on Capitol Hill, when it was a poor, white neighborhood. My grandmother would go down to the old Center Market early in the morning to shop and bargain with the merchants for reduced prices, convincing them that because she was their first customer, a good sale to her would bring them good luck during the day. (Which of us has not used that ploy with merchants elsewhere in the world?) Later I would sometimes drive by one of the houses where my mother was raised. The house has long since been renovated, but a tree from my mother's time still stands in the front yard. I once took her a leaf from the tree before she died.

My father's mother was born in Washington, the child of an Irish mother escaping the potato famine and of an Italian father who came to the United States in the second half of the 1800s to play in the US Marine Band. They both died in the early years of the twentieth century. Their children—my father and his siblings—also lived hard lives on Capitol Hill, with my father leaving school at the age of thirteen to go to work. It is too late to ask where on Capitol Hill they lived.

My parents married in the 1930s and moved to Southeast Washington. Its neighborhoods were filled with primarily working-class families then, but now a recent trend of gentrification has diversified the social classes living in Southeast. As a child, I remember the city as a place of monuments, museums, department stores, and the YWCA (the Young Women's Christian Association), which had a swimming pool where I was forced to take lessons. I remember also segregation when it was expected that blacks would sit in the back of the bus and endure many other indignities, though I was too young at the time to question that.

One of my early childhood memories is of the old nineteenth-century farmhouse my parents rented in Congress Heights (in Southeast DC), and there was nothing but an open field behind us. That house still exists but is now hemmed in by decaying apartment complexes. Few Washingtonians still live in such houses, and the working-class whites who lived in the neighborhood have long since fled the city. But next to the farmhouse is a landmark that still stands— Saint Elizabeths Hospital, built in the nineteenth century for mentally insane residents and veterans. When I lived in the area, the hospital had thousands of patients. Often during the night I could hear some of them screaming in fear of threats real or imagined. Later, my parents were part of the white flight to the suburbs, and they moved out of the city. They were frightened of the downtown area as it deteriorated and crime increased, and they avoided going into the city for the rest of their lives.

My ticket out of my social class was my early love of books and reading. As an only child I had a rather lonesome upbringing. Had my parents had other children, I would perhaps have devoted more time to family events, but instead I buried myself in books. I was always interested in further horizons than I could see from my working-class roots, and reading showed me a bigger world. The rapid expansion of commercial air travel was an important moment during my youth. My mother complained to one of my grade school teachers that, while she was happy I loved to read, I seemed

named) told me that I couldn't marry my first husband *because* he was Iraqi. His objections were based on religious beliefs, I think. At that time, however, being Muslim meant nothing to a Protestant working-class family like mine. As I said, Catholicism was what really worried my parents.

In the 1960s the culture of Washington left much to be desired. It was a bland place with few restaurants, theaters, or concert halls (not that I could afford any of them as a student) and little evident ethnic diversity, though there was a lively black cultural scene that few whites patronized. Apart from government and politics, it was still the sleepy, segregated southern town everyone has written about. I needed to continue expanding my horizons, so I left Washington to explore the world.

After living nearly a decade as a student in Europe and Latin America, I returned to Washington in the 1970s and worked for the government for more than a decade and later taught at my alma mater. I found at first a city still scarred by the race riots of 1968. But by the 1980s, renewal had begun in Washington and ultimately led to what is now the vital city that this book celebrates. If only my parents could experience the city today. At least my son, Doug, a fourth-generation Washingtonian, can live and work in and enjoy this extraordinary place.

So I have written a book about a city that in some profound sense owns me. Some who have read drafts of this book have commented that it is a love letter. It is not intended as such—I am not blind to Washington's blemishes. And I do

The Washington Monument and Lincoln Memorial.
Eric Magnan

not pretend that my Washington is the only Washington. There is the Washington of the poor who struggle for decent lives. There is still the working-class Washington of taxi drivers, delivery and repair people, retailers, and many others working to make ends meet and striving for their children to be the first in their families to attend college as I was in mine. There is the gritty world of crime in DC that George Pelecanos, a prolific local author, has so effectively evoked in his many stories and novels. There is also the "society" of Washington, comprising blacks, Latinos, and whites who attend the balls, society parties, cotillions, and other events—but not often together. I realize that Washington for each of these distinct groups may be different. I have tried to include something of their lives in this book while portraying the city we all share. But in the end, I present the city from my perspective as a middle-class white professional who celebrates this place because of family and familiarity and because I am interested, amused, annoyed, and sometimes inspired by the political theater and intellectual life of Washington, by its diverse and vibrant cultural life, by its expanding amenities, and by its natural beauty, which often, and sometimes unexpectedly, claims my attention and calms my soul.

CHAPTER

2

The History and Politics

WASHINGTON, DC, is a "willed" city. Unlike most other cities, it did not grow out of a center of commerce, a sacred place of worship, or a military encampment. America's Founding Fathers decided to create a new capital in what had been colonial farms and fields and, before that, Native American villages and forests. It was to be a grand city, but it got off to a slow and rocky start. It has faced a number of near-death experiences, including being burned by the British during the War of 1812 and ensuing proposals to move the capital elsewhere, the enormous physical pressures of the Civil War that degraded a still rustic town (generating yet more proposals in Congress to move it elsewhere), and the panoply of assaults on the cityscape in the twentieth century produced by white middle-class flight, the depredations of urban renewal and freeway fundamentalism, the riots of 1968, and the chaos and decline of the early decades of home rule from the 1970s to the 1990s. Astonishingly, Washington has survived each of these trials to become the lively city it is today.

Politics in the capital city—local politics, that is—is equally unusual and part of the broader fabric of American history. Article 1, section 8 of the US Constitution places control of the city in the hands of Congress. For much of its history, that provision meant that local governments were appointed by the president and were accountable to Congress, not to the citizens of the city. Indeed, Washingtonians are still the only Americans who do not have a vote in either the House of Representatives or the Senate. The whys and wherefores of this peculiar situation are a tale unto themselves and are provided in the final section of this chapter.

But we get ahead of our story. So let's start as far back as we can go to recount the history of the place that became Washington, DC.

DC History: First Encounters

The first European to reach what is now the Washington, DC, area was Capt. John Smith in his exploration of the Potomac River in 1608. He describes the Potomac as "fed . . . with many sweet rivers and springs, which fall from the bordering hills. These hills many of them are planted and yeeld no lesse plentie and varietie of fruit, then the river exceedeth with abundance of fish. It is inhabited on both sides."

The fish were so many that he tried to catch them with a frying pan (apparently unsuccessfully). Among the many species of fish then common to the river was the extraordinarily large Atlantic sturgeon (an endangered species today). In the woods along the river were deer, wolves, wild turkeys, wild cats of various kinds, bear, and elk, as well as muskrats, foxes, otters, beavers, and maybe even some buffalo. There were large concentrations of waterfowl, and in addition to birds common today, the area was home to passenger pigeons and Carolina parakeets—now both extinct.

It is estimated that some five thousand Native Americans inhabited the Potomac region below what is now Georgetown. These peoples mainly spoke Algonquin and lived in small villages. The men fished and hunted, and women gathered wood and grew corn, beans, and squash. They made their huts out of reed mats folded over bent saplings, models of which can be visited in Jamestown, Virginia, today.

The Native Americans at the time of the first encounters with Europeans were on the average taller than the Europeans by several inches, probably reflecting a better diet, better hygiene, and a great deal more exercise. One early observer of the Indians of southern Maryland wrote that their character was "noble and cheerful, and they understand well when a matter is proposed to them. . . . They sustain a generous spirit toward everyone; whatever kindness you may confer on them, they return. They decided nothing rashly or seized by a sudden passion, but by reason." But Native Americans were technologically still in the Stone Age with no wheel, no metal (except copper beads), no writing, and no domesticated animals save the dog.

Some of the tribes of the lower Potomac and the western side of the Chesapeake Bay were part of a confederation ruled by Powhatan, the father of the famous Pocahontas who married

By 1790 the area between the Potomac and Anacostia Rivers was held by a number of large landowners, some with manor houses, on properties known as Vineyard and the Rock of Dumbarton (now Georgetown), Rome (below Capitol Hill where Tiber Creek flowed), Blew Playne (Anacostia), Duddington Manor (Capitol Hill and parts of Southeast and Southwest), and Beall's Levels (downtown around the White House). Tobacco cultivation was beginning to decline as the soil deteriorated. Some of the old fields had returned to brush and brambles, but farming in the area continued, managed by some three hundred slaves. Other regions of the landscape that would become part of Washington remained forested. The port town of Georgetown had been established in 1751 and together with Alexandria, farther down the river, created a modest center of trade in the region. The area that would become the nation's capital was a quiet rural backwater.

Creating a Capital

The creation of Washington, DC, was the opening act of a long urban drama that in so many ways echoes the history of the United States and the essential character of the country and its government. It was conceived in politics, designed for the grandeur befitting what was foreseen as a great nation, and constructed in a continuing welter of public parsimony and backbiting, colliding private interests, and constant maneuvering of speculators, opportunists, and ideologues, spiced now and then with corruption and incompetence. But the basic vision of the city remained, and efforts to realize it continued and ultimately prevailed.

The Constitution of the United States was finally ratified in 1788. Even before George Washington was inaugurated as president and before the first federal Congress met in New York City, the issue of where to locate the capital of the new republic was proving to be a difficult and dangerous one. Northerners, especially those from New York City and Philadelphia (where the Continental Congress and Constitutional Convention had met), wanted the capital in one of their cities. There was even some talk of secession in the North if the capital was not established in New York or Pennsylvania.

Southerners, meanwhile, were fearful that if the capital were located in the North, northern interests—especially those commercial and financial interests that would be unfriendly to the South's agrarian, slave-based economies— would control the federal government. Behind these differences was one basic question that arose in many debates on the government's policies over the past two centuries: Should the federal government be large and powerful, actively shaping economic and social conditions in the country, or should it be limited in its size and scope, with greater (but still limited) authorities vested in the individual states? All parties recognized that the decision on where to place the nation's capital, if not handled in a way acceptable to both the North and the South, could break up what was still a very fragile union.

Coincidentally, another major issue in these early months of the republic facilitated the decision on the location of the nation's capital. Debts, left over from the Revolutionary War, remained in the hands of the separate states, many of which were still unpaid and owed to foreign governments. The first secretary of the treasury, Alexander Hamilton, wanted the federal government to assume responsibility for repaying the debts incurred by the former colonies for two reasons—as a means of establishing the creditworthiness of the United States (in case future foreign loans might be needed, for example, to finance a war) and as a way of strengthening the federal government, which would have to impose taxes to finance the debt. Hamilton's proposal was supported by business and financial elites in the North who also wanted a strong, creditworthy central government, but it was opposed by many in the South who feared that such a government was the first step to tyranny (and a loss of the states' rights that protected their way of life) and even perhaps to the reestablishment of monarchy.

These two issues became the basis for a deal that Thomas Jefferson (then secretary of state), Alexander Hamilton, and James Madison (a member of the House of Representatives at the time) made over dinner one evening in 1790 in Manhattan. They agreed that the South would support a federal assumption of debt if the North agreed to locating the national capital on the Potomac River at a place to be chosen by George Washington. Additionally, the capital city would be governed by Congress so as not to leave it under the control of any particular state. This latter condition was written into the US Constitution.

The first president, whose home was located at Mount Vernon on the Virginia side of the Potomac River, was eager to have the capital located in the Potomac valley. His vision of the new capital city was an expansive one. He saw it not only as the center of national politics of a rising nation but also as an important site of commerce, anticipating trade both with Europe through shipping using the Potomac River and Chesapeake Bay and with the territories west of the United States through a series of canals that would be built to link the Potomac with the Ohio River and the territories beyond. Washington also saw the new capital as a place of intellectual endeavor and culture. Having only an eighth grade education himself, Washington's great hope was that a national university would be created in the capital, "where the youth from all parts of the United States might receive the polish of Erudition in the Arts, Sciences and Belle Letters."

George Washington chose a place for the new city just below the falls of the Potomac at the confluence of the Potomac and the Anacostia Rivers. Many agreed that it was a beautiful site with wooded bluffs above the rivers, hills and valleys, and numerous freshwater springs and creeks.

The president turned to the Frenchman Pierre Charles L'Enfant to design the new city. Washington wanted a splendid capital to symbolize the new, democratic republic. Secretary of State Jefferson, who disliked cities, preferred building a smaller town, one appropriate for a government that governed best when it governed least and one that in any case could be established with the very few resources the nation

with it. The main idea for raising the necessary funds for the new city was to purchase building lots from the federal government. Their prices were expected to rise rapidly as the new city took shape and as speculators, hoping to make a quick profit, snapped them up.

But first the local landowners had to be persuaded to deed their property to the government. They would then be paid $67 per acre for any lands used for public buildings or parks. As for the remainder of the lots, the landowners would receive half of the remaining lands, which they could sell, and the federal government would sell the other half to fund construction of the city.

Thus began a prolonged and sordid tale of conflicts between L'Enfant and the three commissioners Washington had appointed to oversee the planning and construction of the town. Tensions grew between the architects of the new buildings, L'Enfant, the commissioners, and the original property owners. L'Enfant failed to produce a plan of the city for potential purchasers of land so they could examine them before the land sales. Botched sales of lots produced little revenue, and building materials for construction did not arrive on time. There were too few workers (even including numerous slaves), many of whom malingered, and what they produced was often shoddy. Several of the land speculators went bankrupt. One ended up in a debtors' prison.

Miraculously, the White House, enough of the Capitol to accommodate Congress, and a number of boardinghouses were habitable by the time Congress and the president moved to Washington in late 1800. But tree trunks still lay where

Thomas Doughty's 1832 view from the old city hall,
Fourth and D Streets.
Library of Congress collections

they had been cut down beside the main roads; building
materials were strewn around the new structures; paths
rather than streets ran between the Capitol and the White
House; large spaces, forests, and empty fields remained; and
a variety of cows, pigs, and sheep grazed here and there.

People sometimes got lost in the woods at night trying to
find their way from one part of town to the other. Abigail
Adams, wife of now President John Adams, observed in 1800
that Washington was "a new country, with houses scattered

over a space of ten miles, and trees & stumps in plenty with, a castle of a house—so I found it. The President's House is in a beautiful situation in front of which is the Potomac with a view of Alexandria. The country around is romantic but a wild, a wilderness at present."

Another observer, the Irish poet Thomas Moore, was less generous. After a visit in 1804, he wrote, "This embryo capital, where Fancy sees / Squares in morasses, obelisks in trees."

Washington's First Near-Death Experience

In August 1814, during the War of 1812, British troops marched into the city, encountering almost no resistance, and burned the Capitol, the White House, and other public buildings. The government's representatives fled on their approach, with First Lady Dolley Madison leaving a recently prepared dinner on the table in the White House (British officers ate it before torching the building). She did manage to retrieve Gilbert Stuart's famous portrait of George Washington, a copy of which still hangs in the East Room of the White House.

In the city's first near-death experience, the burning of the capital led to proposals in Congress to move the capital back to Philadelphia. By only a handful of votes, Congress finally decided not to do so and appropriated $500,000 (a substantial sum in those days) for rebuilding the city. This time that feat was accomplished in only three years. The city was, however, still more rural than urban, a place of boulevards that turned from dust into mud when it rained. Houses remained

George Munger's 1814 painting of the White House
after the British torched it.
Library of Congress collections

few and far between. The canal for Tiber Creek was built but
soon silted up and turned into an unwholesome, often swampy
drainage ditch. The city's summers were hot and humid (as
they are today), and the lower elevations experienced wide-
spread "ague and fever" (mostly malaria) with occasional
outbreaks of yellow fever, typhoid, and cholera and vague
maladies such as "bilious fever."

Nevertheless, the city began slowly to take shape. Houses
and shops filled in the border of Pennsylvania Avenue and
around Capitol Hill and the White House. A few churches
were established. St. John's Episcopal, for example, facing
Lafayette Square in front of the White House, was founded

in 1815 and still holds services. Several markets were also built, with the largest being the Center Market (called early on the Marsh Market because of its site next to Tiber Creek) on the south side of Pennsylvania Avenue and backing on the Mall, where the National Archives are now. Beginning in 1801, the US Marine Band provided music on official occasions, and the Washington Theater opened in 1804 to host a variety of visiting performers, plays, and operas. It was replaced by the National Theatre in 1835. After multiple fires in the nineteenth century, the reconstructed National Theatre continues to operate today. Washington, however, was hardly a town and certainly not a seat of culture during these early years of its existence. Funding for improvements in the city remained limited with Congress reluctant to put up the money and with the city prohibited by law from taxing federal property. Lacking much industry or commerce, the city's tax base also remained small.

In 1836 Washington received an offer of $500,000 from the estate of the late British scientist James Smithson to build the Smithsonian Institution "for the increase and diffusion of knowledge." This extraordinary gift set off several lively debates. Should the United States accept funds from a foreigner, especially from a citizen of the former colonial power, which many still resented? Did the Constitution permit the federal government to accept such a gift and potentially eclipse the powers of the individual states? Once the government decided to accept the gift, it debated what to do with the money: Establish the national university that George Washington had dreamed of? Or fund public schools, of which there were few? Or set up a research institution? Or perhaps build an expanded national library? Finally in 1846, it was decided not to build a national university but to found the Smithsonian Institution as a trust and allow its secretary and board of regents to decide exactly what the institution would do. Ten years later, in what is now called the Castle—the earliest Smithsonian building built on the Mall looks like a medieval European castle—the foundation offered lectures, exhibits, publications, and support for research by US scientists. It was an important and fortuitous step toward making Washington a place of intellectual endeavor as both George Washington and Thomas Jefferson had hoped. The Smithsonian Institution is now the largest museum and research complex in the world.

What did not develop in Washington, contrary to the hopes of the first president, was commercial activity. He had been active in creating the Patowmack Company to build a canal from Washington around the rapids of Great Falls and northwestward to attract trade from the Ohio Valley via the Potomac River. That company was later taken over by the Chesapeake and Ohio Canal Company, which built a canal 183 miles to Cumberland, Maryland. However, with the development of much more rapid and efficient rail transport (that did more to link Baltimore than Washington to the country's interior), the canal was obsolete before it was completed. George Washington's dream of a commercial capital to supplement his political capital remained out of reach.

Foreign visitors to the United States began putting Washington on their itineraries. Many were not impressed with what they saw. Charles Dickens, who visited the city in 1842, famously called Washington a "City of Magnificent Intentions. . . . Spacious avenues, that begin in nothing and lead nowhere; streets, mile-long, that only want houses, roads and inhabitants; public buildings that need but a public to be complete; and ornaments of great thoroughfares, which only lack great thoroughfares to ornament." But some saw not how far Washington fell short of its ambitions but the magnificence of those ambitions and the progress being made toward realizing them. A decade earlier, Fanny Trollope, author of *Domestic Manners of the Americans*, commented that "the appearance of the metropolis rising gradually into life and splendour, is a spectacle of high historic interest." She added, "The total absence of all sights, sounds, or smells of commerce, adds greatly to the charm."

By the Civil War, the population of the city had grown to seventy-five thousand inhabitants. Nearly sixty-one thousand were white, fourteen thousand were black, and of the black inhabitants, three thousand were slaves. It was a city of striking contrasts that housed political transients and permanent residents, some of whom were very affluent and many very poor. Washington was a symbol of liberty but had a sizable slave population, and, until 1850, slave traders operated within view of the Capitol. While it boasted two of the most magnificent buildings in America—the Capitol and the White House—it still had unpaved streets, no sewer system, and animals grazing in vacant lots and in roadways all over town. The city had an impressive museum system in the Smithsonian Institution and an embryonic cultural life, but it still had few public schools (albeit a number of private academies existed).

Behind these contrasts were several conditions that were unique to Washington and some that reflected widely held American attitudes. Americans wanted grandeur in their capital city but did not want to pay for it, and members of Congress, who typically spent time in the city only when Congress was in session and left their families at home, were not interested in appropriating funds for projects that did not benefit their constituents. Further, the city itself had no vote in Congress to further its own interests there. And with its limited tax base, the city could do little to finance its needs for infrastructure and services. To add to its problems, Washington had become an attractive place for immigrants and, above all, free blacks (and fleeing slaves) who hoped for work and, in the latter case, better treatment than they would receive in the rest of the South given the presence of the federal government. Most of these immigrants were poor, often illiterate, and unemployed, adding to an already large number of impoverished Washingtonians. Finally, attitudes in the first half of the nineteenth century on what role the government should play in the economy, especially in the South, were quite different from those of today. People still considerably resisted funding many of the public services such as schools, minimal health facilities, and even adequate firefighting and police forces that we now take for granted. So Washington, DC, on the brink of the Civil War was still a small, raw, and sleepy Southern town. No one could foresee what the coming rupture between the North and the South would do to the city.

George Cooke's 1834 painting of Washington, DC,
from across the Anacostia River.
The White House Historical Association

The Civil War and Afterward

Wars and major national crises often destroy cities. But they
can also make cities, especially capital cities, larger and more
prosperous and more vibrant. The Civil War had an enormous
impact on Washington, DC. In a second near-death experience for the city, the war caused its population to balloon,
degraded its limited infrastructure, and nearly resulted in its
demise as the nation's capital. But eventually, the consequences

of the war led to improvements that began to turn Washington from a struggling, unhealthy village to the respectable and handsome capital that George Washington and Pierre L'Enfant had envisioned.

Otto von Bismarck, chancellor of Germany in the late nineteenth century, is said to have remarked that "God has a special providence for fools, drunks, and the United States of America." Surely it was a special providence that Abraham Lincoln was sworn in as president in March 1861, as the South was preparing to secede from the Union. Lincoln proved unwavering in his commitment to preserve the Union through a far longer and bloodier war than anyone had imagined.

Washington, as the seat of government, was naturally the focal point of the war effort. This meant that the city was soon inundated with large numbers of soldiers and job seekers as well as blacks fleeing slavery and violence in the South. Initially, soldiers slept in the Capitol, the Treasury Department, the Patent Office, and tents wherever there were open spaces. The basement of the Capitol became a bakery to supply food for the flood of soldiers. Later many buildings were turned into hospitals as the casualties of war flooded the city.

Soldiers also influenced the town in other ways. With time on their hands, many of them frequented neighborhoods such as "Joe Hooker's Division," just south of where the Treasury Department now stands, with its bars and bordellos. Local lore has it that the area was named for Gen. Joe Hooker, who reportedly gathered a group of prostitutes there for the benefit of his soldiers (and to keep an eye on the shenanigans of his boys).

Poor blacks tended to locate in the "Island," an area of slums in the southwest of the city framed by the Washington Canal; in "Murder Bay," where the Commerce Department sits today; and in shanties in the back alleys all over the city. Some poor whites, mainly a concentration of Irish immigrants, had already occupied an area near the Capitol called Swampoodle—the site of what is now Union Station—so named because of the swamps and puddles that formed there after a heavy rain. These imaginative descriptives have long been lost with the many changes that occurred in Washington in the twentieth century, leaving a nicer city but far fewer evocative neighborhood names.

In addition to the number of people drawn to the city during the war, Washington's southern location increased tensions in the city. Surrounded by Virginia, which eventually joined the Confederacy, and Maryland, which teetered for a while on the brink of secession, Washington was extremely vulnerable to attack by Confederate armies, especially at the beginning of the war. Conditions were so threatening that Lincoln arrived in Washington surreptitiously for his inauguration because of credible rumors that there would be an assassination attempt against him as his train passed through Maryland.

In 1864 Confederate troops from Gen. Jubal Early's army did attack the city and got as far as Silver Spring on its northern outskirts before they were repulsed. Although many of the capital's residents were sympathetic to the South and actually decamped to the Confederacy at the beginning of the war, the city also had its share of spies and rumors of spies and conspiracies.

While the Civil War saw the population of the city more than triple between 1860 and 1865 (rising to an estimated 200,000) and some accompanying increase in housing and economic development, little was done to improve the amenities of life. Most streets remained unpaved. On the Mall, one found cattle pens and slaughterhouses beside the unfinished stump of the Washington Monument and train tracks below the Capitol running to a station located where the National Gallery of Art now stands. Sanitation was still primitive. People often dumped sewage and refuse into the alleys or into the Washington Canal, which subsequently backed up when the tide came in. The smells pervading Washington in the summertime of that era can hardly be imagined. Moreover, private wells, long the major source of water, were often contaminated. Not surprising, disease stalked the city. Typhoid fever even killed Abraham Lincoln's young son Willie.

Despite the stresses of war and all the discomforts plaguing the capital, the great poet Walt Whitman, who spent much of the Civil War in Washington tending to wounded soldiers, still saw flashes of beauty and promise here. In February 1863 he penned the following:

> I wander about a good deal, sometimes at night under the moon. To-night took a long look at the President's house. The white portico—the palace-like, tall, round columns, spotless as snow—the walls also—the tender and soft

moonlight, flooding the pale marble, and making peculiar faint languishing shades, not shadows—everywhere a soft transparent hazy, thin, blue moon-lace, hanging in the air . . . everything so white, so marbly pure and dazzling, yet soft—the White House of future poems, and of dreams and dramas.

The city of Washington also has the important distinction of emancipating slaves prior to the 1863 Emancipation Proclamation. On April 16, 1862, President Lincoln signed the Compensated Emancipation Act freeing slaves in Washington. This day is still celebrated locally.

During the Civil War, Washington became the center of the enormous and ultimately successful Union war effort. By the war's end in 1865, it had become the capital city of a much more unified nation with a much more powerful national government. But the city itself was degraded, crowded, and unhealthy.

A Third Near-Death Experience

Nevertheless, in the years after the Civil War, neither Congress nor the city government took action to address the pressing problems of the town. Both lacked the resources, and as in the past, Congress appeared not to have any interest in bettering the city. Soon proposals began to appear in Congress and the media to move the capital to the Midwest (not surprising, these proposals came from representatives of Kansas, Missouri, Ohio, and elsewhere in the heartland). This debate was a source of rising concern to Washingtonians.

In 1866 Congress passed a bill providing for the immediate enfranchisement of blacks as part of Reconstruction policies after the war. The city elections in the following two years resulted in a number of blacks gaining political office. By 1870 the city had passed civil rights laws prohibiting discrimination against blacks in restaurants, hotels, theaters, and elsewhere. Prominent blacks even attended the second inaugural ball of President Ulysses S. Grant. Washington at this time was very forward leaning in its laws governing race relations.

But most of these advances proved short lived. In 1871 some members of Congress were none too pleased with the rise of black political power in Washington. They voted to change the existing municipal government and replace it with a "territorial government" led by a governor with a council, which was appointed by the president; an elected House of Delegates; and a nonvoting member of Congress. These changes substantially reduced the voice of Washingtonians in their own governance.

But they also did something else. The most important change shaped the development of Washington by creating a board of public works, with five members appointed by the president, to undertake much-needed improvements in the city. The improvements would be paid for with local taxes and bond issues, but there were limitations on how much public debt could be assumed. Although no one knew it at the time, the stage was set for a revolution in Washington's physical appearance.

Among the five board members appointed by President Grant was Alexander Robey "Boss" Shepherd (who is profiled in more detail in chapter 5). A hard-driving man who soon assumed leadership of the board, Shepherd quickly produced an ambitious plan for making improvements in the city, including creating a sewage system; grading, paving, and lighting the streets; planting trees; and filling in the wretched Washington Canal. Not one to wait for the niceties of planning details to be worked out, Shepherd commenced work on his projects all at once. Where he met resistance to his plans from powerful individuals, he found a way to go around them and did not let them stop him.

Despite legal challenges, uncertain financing, and problems in the execution of Shepherd's plan, by 1873 the improvements in the city's amenities were striking enough for people to begin talking of a "new Washington." There was no more talk of relocating the nation's capital to the Midwest. But Congress, extremely irritated at the huge debt it was left to pay, decided in 1874 to replace the territorial government with one run by three presidentially appointed commissioners and agreed to share the expenses of running the city. It effectively abolished what was left of home rule.

With the growing power of the federal government, the symbolism and prominence of the city led to the first major political demonstration held there—the arrival of Coxey's "army" in 1894. Protesting the loss of jobs and the ongoing depression at that time, five hundred men, led by the populist businessman Jacob Coxey, marched from Ohio to Washington only to be arrested and dispersed on the Capitol grounds. This "army" left the phrase "enough food to feed Coxey's army" in my parents' vocabulary, passed down to them no doubt by their parents, some of whom were living in Washington at that time. Coxey's men held the first demonstration in the city, but many would occur in the coming century and beyond.

Washington in the Twentieth Century

The last quarter of the nineteenth century saw a real estate boom in Washington, with new areas opening up in the northern part of the city reached by streetcar transport. During this Gilded Age, families that had become rich elsewhere in the country migrated to Washington to join the social elite and enjoy the seasons of balls, dinners, and a host of other activities. They built themselves vast mansions in the West End along Massachusetts Avenue and in the Dupont Circle area, a number of which still stand (and many now house embassies and private clubs).

Important public works undertaken at this time included completing the Washington Monument in 1884. Construction on it had commenced in 1848 but was halted in 1854 as a result of political wrangling and through the Civil War owing to a lack of resources. When building started up again in 1876, the color of the marble in the already built section could not be matched with similar stone. Thus the final three-fourths of the monument is a different shade of white today. At this time the Library of Congress was also constructed, and the mud flats on the Potomac behind the White House were filled in. Additionally, the National Zoo and Rock Creek Park, the forest that runs through the western part of the city, were established.

By the end of the nineteenth century, Washington had become an attractive, pleasant city and the capital of a rapidly industrializing economy and rising world power. Perhaps because industrialization was taking place in other cities but not in Washington, the city was also seen as "a city at rest and peace." In the words of a visiting Englishman, the city had "an air of comfort, of leisure, of space to spare, of stateliness you hardly expected in America. It looks the sort of place where nobody has to work for his living, or, at any rate, not hard." The first part of this observation may still be true; the last part is surely not today, lingering myths of a lazy bureaucracy notwithstanding. But more on that later.

Comfort and stateliness were not for everyone in Washington. It was also a city of very poor people, many of them African Americans, who continued to migrate to Washington to escape the deepening racial exclusion in the South. The poor were typically hidden out of sight in tenements and crowded shacks in fetid alleys behind the great houses of the city. In 1897 nearly nineteen thousand people, mostly black— or one in twelve Washingtonians—lived in more than three hundred places with names like Pork Steak Alley, Slop Bucket Row, or even, perhaps ironically, Hope Avenue. Furthermore, over the last quarter of the nineteenth century and the first half of the twentieth century, the civil rights that African Americans had gained were extinguished. Jim Crow laws segregating blacks and whites in nearly all walks of life were tightened, even to the extent that black and white civil servants working for the same office were required to work and eat in different rooms.

Segregation in Washington provoked the great blues musician Huddie "Lead Belly" Ledbetter to write a song about the city called "The Bourgeois Blues."

But the black community in Washington was large and dynamic enough—with its own middle class—to create a parallel black universe with its own shops, churches, schools (several of which were at least as good as white schools), civic associations, and social clubs. Howard University—the

Theodore R. Davis's sketch of a nearly finished
Howard University, circa 1870.
Historical Society of Washington, DC

nation's greatest black university—was established in 1867 and soon became a focal point of black education and intellectual endeavor. During the first half of the twentieth century, the liveliest cultural scene in the city was the black one, with its music and prominent musicians, including the great Duke Ellington; entertainers; poets; and clubs. U Street, along the north edge of the Old City, became known as the Black Broadway. It wasn't Harlem, but it was vibrant and famous.

The early twentieth century was a time of change and reform in the United States. The country emerged victorious from the Spanish-American War in 1898, proud of itself and its accomplishments and recognized as a rising world power. Meanwhile, at home, the consequences of rapid industrialization and urbanization and the impact of the severe depression of 1893 fed the Progressive Movement, which aimed to establish a wide range of societal reforms. The period also saw changes in people's attitudes toward cities—how they should be planned and how the destitution and squalor evident in many American cities might be reduced.

The "City Beautiful" Movement had gained much attention at this time. This approach to city planning ensured that the central core of a city had parks and open space, a coherent architecture, and an aesthetically pleasing landscape that created a harmonious and orderly environment. It was hoped that beautifying cities would produce more effective social control, especially involving the poor. The leaders hoped to imbue the poor with more civic pride, greater responsibility, and a moral improvement that would lead them out of pov-

erty. The idea that beauty could lead people out of poverty
seems today wildly naive, but the world was a newer place a
century ago and was struggling with massive social changes
that had never been experienced.

Washington, DC, was the first place where the City Beautiful Movement had an impact on city planning. At the urging
of the American Institute of Architects, Senator James
McMillan, chairman of the Senate's Committee on the District of Columbia, created the Senate Park Improvement
Commission in 1900 (soon called the McMillan Commission) and included fifteen of the nation's best-known architects. They were to make recommendations for renewing the
historic center of the city, including the Mall and the areas
around the Capitol and Pennsylvania Avenue. At the time,
Murder Bay still thrived south of Pennsylvania Avenue. Train
tracks crossed the Mall, a large train terminal sat on one side
of it, and in 1901, Congress had ceded yet more property in
the center of the Mall for the Pennsylvania Railroad's future
use. The Park Commission was tasked with determining how
Washington should look as the capital city of a powerful
country—one whose beauty and magnificence could eventually rival that of European cities.

The commission delivered its report in 1901. Its basic
intent was as much as possible to return the core of the city
to Pierre L'Enfant's original plan, with its wide boulevards,
open spaces, long views, and stately buildings. Over the ensuing several decades, many of the commission's recommendations were enacted. First among the changes implemented as
a result of the McMillan Commission's work was the removal

of the train station and train tracks on the Mall. A new train station, today's Union Station, was built north of the Capitol and replaced the shanties of Swampoodle.

Eventually emerging from the McMillan Commission's work were other important improvements in the monumental core of Washington. Many of the slums near the center of the city, often within view of the Capitol, were cleared, though history does not tell us what happened to the people who had been living in them. A number of new federal buildings were constructed along Pennsylvania Avenue in what is now the Federal Triangle, replacing Murder Bay. The Tidal Basin was created with a beach for swimming and eventually was bordered by several thousand Japanese cherry trees. A series of parks, based on the old Civil War forts surrounding Washington, took shape. Rock Creek Park was cleaned up, and a number of elegant new bridges built over Rock Creek facilitated transport between Georgetown and the city. The Lincoln Memorial was opened in 1924. In short, much of the civic architecture of the city was constructed in the first thirty years of the twentieth century.

The two world wars of the twentieth century also had an impact on Washington. An influx of people working for a rapidly expanding government put intense pressure on housing and on office space. During both world wars, temporary offices were constructed on the Mall, with the last ones removed only in 1972. Many of those people coming to the city to work stayed after the wars were over and added to the demand for homes. It must be noted, however, that owing to the racist hiring policies President Wilson enacted during his tenure, he oversaw a declining number of African Americans employed by the federal government. The federal government had previously been a key source of employment for Washington's African American population, thus Wilson's policy had a significant impact on the community.

The introduction first of horse-drawn trams after the Civil War and then of electric trolleys in the late nineteenth and early twentieth centuries made it possible for government workers to live farther and farther from the town's center and commute to work. As a result, by 1940, not only was L'Enfant's Old City filled in but much of the District of Columbia as well, pushing to the official borders of the capital and into Maryland and Virginia. As residents moved out of the downtown area, many of Washington's older houses and hotels, some of them historic and some magnificent, were demolished and replaced with modern office buildings.

But, much as it did in other American cities, the automobile had the greatest impact on the evolution of Washington in the second half of the twentieth century. By 1950 many Americans could afford cars, and many who lived in the cities opted to move to the suburbs for larger houses and greater space. They also fled to the suburbs to avoid school integration after the Supreme Court's ruling in 1954 of *Brown v. the Board of Education* desegregating public schools. Beginning at mid-century, white flight drove down the population numbers in Washington. And as more middle-and working-class whites abandoned the city, especially the close-in neighborhoods, those areas decayed from poverty, neglect, and crime. Retail department stores downtown found it harder to stay afloat as suburbanites made their purchases in local malls. The city's tax base shrank just as the needs for increased expenditures in a deteriorating city rose.

A Fourth Near-Death Experience

In the mid-twentieth century, two popular approaches emerged to address the problems of congestion and decaying neighborhoods in Washington and other American cities—urban renewal and what I call freeway fundamentalism. The focus of urban renewal in Washington centered on Southwest, the home of some twenty-four thousand working-class and poor people, four-fifths of whom were African Americans. Many of their houses lacked electricity and plumbing. But rather than trying to rehabilitate the existing houses, the Redevelopment Land Agency (a federal agency in charge of ridding Washington of urban decay) took a radical modernist approach to city planning: demolish old structures and replace them with modern buildings. Thus, the population was forced to relocate, an area of more than 550 acres was razed, and new houses and apartments for the middle class were built along with shopping facilities. This urban renewal project certainly got rid of a great number of slums and poor people. It also destroyed established communities as residents were dispersed. Further, it demolished so much housing stock, some of it pleasant, some of it historic, and nearly all of it for low-income populations. Old black Washingtonians who used to live in Southwest still remember their neighborhood with painful nostalgia. By the end of the renewal project, the area was home to nearly 90 percent white, middle-class families.

The freeway fundamentalists posed an even greater threat to the integrity of Washington and its urban fabric. Traffic congestion in the area was growing with the increasing numbers of suburbanites driving their cars to work in the city. The troubled public bus and streetcar system, shaken by strikes against segregation on the streetcars, was not adequate to handle the congestion, and most drivers preferred the comfort and flexibility of their own vehicles. Some saw increased rapid rail transport as an answer. Others preferred freeways, which would permit cars to enter and leave cities quickly and conveniently and reduce traffic tie-ups. And the federal government was willing to pay 90 percent of the cost of construction of freeways. The transportation engineers of the DC Department of Highways were eager to plan the city's freeways. They came up with the idea of an Inner Loop expressway, or a linked set of limited-access, multiple-lane freeways mostly in open or covered cuts belowground that would continue through the downtown area. The freeways would run a long semicircle from Virginia through Southwest and Southeast, go past the Capitol for ten blocks to the Anacostia River, then make a 180-degree turn north and west, run back toward Virginia through a number of close-in neighborhoods in Northwest, and exit on a new bridge across the Potomac above Georgetown. Connecting this long loop, they envisioned another freeway that would run in front of the Capitol, creating a figure eight. Several spurs would link the freeway to highways leading out of town toward the north, east, and south.

In 1959 when a report by the National Capital Planning Commission recommending the Inner Loop was published, residents of some of the more affluent neighborhoods through which the freeways would be cut rose up in opposition. The proposed freeways not only would affect the value of their properties but also would likely devastate their communities, dividing and isolating areas, discouraging the pedestrian traffic that the shops and restaurants relied on, and creating noise and pollution. Many being successful lawyers, opponents of the idea organized themselves, created information campaigns, lobbied, went to court to block the freeways, and raised the issue of rapid rail transport as an alternative. Thus began a long battle between proponents of the freeways and proponents of a subway system that involved the citizens of Washington, the highway lobby, the DC government, the transportation planners, the members of Congress, and the White House.

Part of the Inner Loop system was actually built through parts of Northwest, Southwest, and Southeast (on elevated freeways) and along the front of the Capitol (underground). The rest of the Loop intended for Northwest Washington was not built. The freeways that were constructed had exactly the impact that its opponents feared: Their "tangle of high speed roads, interrupted streets, institutional scale and absence of street life . . . disrupts the area's urban fabric," according to one description of them in the 2008 National Capital Framework Plan. However, out of the battle over freeways came the Washington Metro (subway) system, which was to become a major advance in public transport for the city and its environs—and later a source of dissatisfaction due to performance and safety concerns.

Redevelopment and freeways were not the only limitations on the quality of life in the city. Theaters (except cinemas), concert halls, good restaurants, and other amenities remained limited in number. White society amused itself at exclusive clubs and dinner parties, while members of black society, stratified by color and wealth, had their own private clubs. Not surprising, the whites' flight to the suburbs was soon joined by the flight of the rising black middle class. Pennsylvania Avenue, part of the decaying downtown area, was shabby enough in the early 1960s to cause newly inaugurated President Kennedy to urge that it be rehabilitated. (The Pennsylvania Avenue Redevelopment Corporation was later established in 1972 to do just that.) Little wonder that Kennedy famously described Washington as a city "with Northern charm and Southern efficiency."

The remaining decades of the twentieth century brought yet more trials for the city. After Dr. Martin Luther King Jr. was assassinated in Memphis, Tennessee, in April 1968, Washington and many other American cities with large black communities and increasingly assertive black activists erupted in riots that led to looting and burning lasting several days.

The riots of April 1968 left a tremendous and terrible mark on the city and shaped the lives of a generation of Washingtonians. Demonstrations began at Fourteenth and U Streets with people venting their anger over the assassination of Dr. King and the response of local businesses. Demonstration leaders wanted businesses to close down as they had done when President Kennedy was assassinated in November 1963. Protests quickly devolved, however, into rioting, looting, and wanton destruction. Many shops and businesses in the close-in areas, most of which were in African American neighborhoods, were destroyed. It seemed that all the anger of two centuries of oppression bubbled up and expressed itself along the U Street corridor for several days that spring.

The riots altered the behavior and relationships between many Washingtonians. The riots further hastened suburban flight and the deepening blight of a number of downtown areas. Many jobs were lost, and the downtown shopping experience wilted, both from a lack of options and a sense that the city had changed. Folks living in the suburbs didn't want to go downtown anymore. Businesses were slow to return to the U Street corridor. In many cases, decades passed following the riots before new businesses opened their doors. Though many middle-class African Americans fled Washington after the riots, the remaining community became an important place during the post–civil rights era for the African American empowerment movement.

The riots in Washington occurred during the period in which civil rights issues were high on the national political agenda. Also on that agenda, at least in the mind of President Lyndon Johnson and many of the city's residents, was regaining home rule for the District of Columbia. As it had been for nearly a century, commissioners appointed by the president still governed the city. In 1965 a home rule bill was defeated in Congress after many members of Congress from the South and the Greater Washington Board of Trade, representing white business interests, opposed it. Johnson then offered another bill in 1967 that would allow a partial move toward home rule, and Congress approved it. Under the new regulations, the president would appoint a city council and mayor or commissioner while Congress would continue to control the city's budget and could block any locally promulgated laws. Johnson appointed Walter Washington, a black housing official who had worked in Washington and New York, as mayor/commissioner.

In 1969 District residents elected their own school board for the first time, and in 1971 they elected a nonvoting delegate to Congress. With the chairmanship of the key Committee on District of Columbia changing from a Southern Democrat, who opposed home rule, to a supportive African American congressman (Charles Diggs of Michigan), a home rule bill finally passed Congress, and President Richard Nixon signed it in 1973. Home rule was not complete, however. Political compromises to gain enough votes in Congress meant that the appointment of judges remained in the president's hands, and Congress still had the power to approve the city's budget and could veto any of its laws. Furthermore, Washington's member of Congress still did not have a vote in that body.

Limited home rule was in itself an important advance for the city. But it brought its own problems. The first elected mayor was Walter Washington, a moderate who implemented little change in both the personnel running the city (mostly white) and the city's fiscally conservative policies. It fell to his successor, Marion Barry, to alter the political fabric of Washington, DC.

The son of a sharecropper from Mississippi, Marion Shepilov Barry Jr. nearly completed a PhD in chemistry and became a civil rights activist. Flamboyant and sometimes defiant, he also knew how to conciliate and charm when necessary. After becoming mayor in 1979, Barry's tenure in office was controversial, and many of his appointments, especially in his later terms, were based on patronage and whim rather than capability. Further, weak oversight within the Barry administrations led to a deterioration in public services. Charges of corruption grew, and the mayor himself was eventually caught on videotape and arrested and jailed for cocaine use. But he remained highly popular with many in the city, and after his release from prison, he served on the city council and was elected mayor for a fourth term in 1994. During this term the city became virtually bankrupt, and Congress imposed a financial control board to manage the city's finances—a blow, albeit temporary, to home rule in Washington and to the reputation of the city itself.

But there was worse to come. During the Barry administration, Washington suffered from a crack cocaine epidemic, as did many other American cities. Washington already had a problem with heroin addiction, but crack proved attractive to a broader population, including poor youth and low-income workers as well as middle-class professionals. It was relatively cheap, and the pleasure it reportedly produced was quick and often addictive. Accompanying the crack epidemic was a crime epidemic; both proved challenging to a police force weakened by controversy before and during the Barry administrations. By the early 1990s, Washington was being called the murder capital of the United States, fueling a continuing decline in population. By 2000 the population of the city was 25 percent less than it had been in 1960.

Turn Around

Even it its darkest days in the last third of the twentieth century, the seeds of Washington's revitalization had been planted and were beginning to bear fruit. In 1958 Congress had passed legislation to create a National Cultural Center, which would be funded by private donations. President Kennedy helped raise funds for the center during his presidency, but it was only after his death in 1963 that Congress agreed to appropriate $23 million toward the construction of the $70 million facility and to memorialize it with the president's name. When it opened in 1971, the John F. Kennedy Center for the Performing Arts, with its theaters for concerts, opera, and stage performances, added important venues for various productions in Washington.

The Kennedy Center marked the beginning of a real expansion in the cultural offerings of the city. Just one story shows how a great performing arts facility can encourage arts generally. One of the best choral groups in Washington is the Gay Men's Chorus. This group was formed after enthusiasts attended a 1981 performance at the Kennedy Center by the

Gay Men's Chorus from San Francisco. Its members encouraged leaders of Washington's local gay community to form their own singing group, which draws its own large crowds today.

Since the establishment of the Kennedy Center, the performing arts scene in the city has become much larger and more diverse with the creation of new theaters and resident theater companies. Washington reportedly has the fourth-largest theater scene among US cities—behind New York, Chicago, and Los Angeles—a lively array of music of all kinds, and organizations incubating new performing artists and theater and music companies. The community of exhibition artists—painters, photographers, and sculptors—has also begun to expand in the city and its surrounding suburbs. No one would mistake the art scene in Washington for that of New York, but it is now so much richer than it was in the last quarter of the twentieth century. And as we explore in greater detail in a later chapter, it is unusually diverse, with performing artists appealing to the variety of ethnic groups that are now part of the Washington community.

The subway system that emerged from the fight over freeways is another essential element in the revitalization of Washington. The gradually expanding network of stations eased travel within the city and to and from it for suburban commuters. But most important, stations began to act as poles of development, stimulating investment and growth around them with new shops, rehabilitated housing, and a livelier street life.

Other major infrastructure investments that contributed to the city's revitalization included the restoration of Union Station, which had deteriorated badly during the 1960s. It reopened in 1988 as not just a train station but also a shopping mall, food court, and grand public space. A new convention center opened in 1983 in a formerly run-down area of downtown, with hotels and shops soon appearing nearby. By the end of the century, that convention center was obsolete, blown up—demolished by the government, not by terrorists—and replaced by another, larger one farther north in another previously run-down area of the city. This neighborhood now shows strong signs of revitalization.

There are two places in Washington where residents of all classes and races come together. One is in the DC courts, where all residents are called on to serve jury duty. It is very difficult for any DC resident to get a pass on this civic duty simply because of his or her elevated political position. Even the mayor is summoned for jury duty every two years. My son received his first summons at sixteen years of age! It is truly unavoidable. The other place residents gather is at major sporting events. The city is especially obsessed with the Redskins, its professional football team. Alas, it does not enjoy many winning seasons, and its owner is caught up in a dispute over the alleged racial overtones of the team's name. Other popular sports include basketball (professional and collegiate); professional soccer; ice hockey, with the occasionally successful Capitals and their great star Alex Ovechkin; and baseball. In 2005 the Montreal-run franchise moved to

Washington and became the Nationals, bringing major league baseball to the city for the first time in several decades.

The Verizon Center—a sports center for basketball, hockey, popular concerts, and other events—was opened in 1997 in the dilapidated area just north of Pennsylvania Avenue where the 1968 riots had left a badly damaged neighborhood. Within a decade of the complex's opening, the neighborhood, now called Penn Quarter, had become one of the most vibrant and busiest places in the city, with new shops, theaters, restaurants, museums, and condominiums (but at the cost of a decline in the city's nearby minuscule Chinatown). The rapidity of the change was stunning to longtime Washingtonians, including myself. Another major sports facility, a new baseball stadium, was opened in 2008 in Southeast near the Anacostia River. Nationals Park led to a revitalization of that area as well.

Though this city is obsessed with sports, particularly with the Redskins, even this part of the city culture has been altered by income inequality and gentrification. In the old Redskins Stadium, named after Robert F. Kennedy, fans of all strata of society would often sit together. Now ticket affordability and luxury seating options in the capacious home of the Redskins, FedEx Field, has altered the way in which Washingtonians interact at sporting events.

The revival of downtown and close-in Washington as a mixed-use, lived-in city has been based on more than a new subway, entertainment facilities, and sports stadiums. Deeper changes are at work. One was the subsidence in the 1990s of the crack cocaine epidemic. For reasons that are not well understood, crack cocaine began losing popularity in the mid-1990s, and accompanying the trend, crime rates dropped in half by 2007.

After the city declined in the 1960s, numerous efforts over the decades by the federal government, the DC government, redevelopment commissions, Washington business enterprises, philanthropic foundations, and local communities all contributed to the city's continuing revitalization. For example, community development corporations were organized to mobilize local interest in neighborhood improvements, to seek funding to upgrade housing (including low-income housing) and street fronts, and to find philanthropists who would fund facilities to benefit the community and investors who would start new businesses in the area. Residents also lobbied the DC government to place a subway stop in their area or to make other community investments. Soon professionals looking to live in town began to buy and renovate dilapidated housing, giving a boost to real estate prices and attracting others looking for homes.

My family once bought a renovated house on a run-down street in the middle of town. We experienced the opportunistic crime common in such areas with break-ins, we heard noisy prostitutes shouting to each other on street corners during warm summer evenings, and we learned about drug busts and murders in the alley behind our house. We were also aware of racial tension and perhaps a bit of hostility toward us given that we were white and relatively well off and the long-term residents were black and not well-to-do. They must have guessed how their neighborhood was set to change. But many of our neighbors, even the prostitutes, were also friendly and kind and often very helpful to us.

In many cases, members of Washington's large gay community were the first to move into formerly depressed areas. Once new investors or house buyers began to move in, shops and amenities would expand, thus attracting more investors and house buyers. In short, revitalization became market driven. This process of revitalization continues to sweep across the city, from west to east and outward from Capitol Hill.

These trends are evident in other cities as well, reflecting perhaps a more fundamental change in American society and culture. The twentieth-century obsession with suburban living appears to be giving way to a "new urbanism," with people expressing a desire for more street life. They want to live in a varied community of residences and commercial establishments where they can walk to shops, to entertainment, to others' houses, and even to work—the kind of urban living urged by Jane Jacobs, the author of *The Death and Life of American Cities* (one of the great and most influential books on cities of the twentieth century). The racial fears of earlier decades that helped drive whites out of towns to the suburbs seem also to have diminished, especially among young professionals, both black and white. Census data on a number of older American cities, such as Atlanta, Baltimore, Boston, Detroit, Milwaukee, and Minneapolis, that had been losing population during the latter part of the twentieth century show that by 2005, they had begun to grow again also.

All of these changes, beginning in the difficult years of the latter half of the 1900s, are already making Washington, DC, a city not only of political theater and of symbolism and grandeur but also a livable and walkable city. In fact, one student of cities recently judged Washington to be the most walkable of major American cities.

But as a city, Washington is far from perfect. The revitalization described here is the other side of gentrification, where better-off individuals and families buy into poor neighborhoods, leading to an increase in real estate prices, rents, and local taxes. The result is that many poorer residents are forced out, and with low-income housing being scarce downtown, they have to relocate more and more distant from the city center, with all the attendant pain of dislocation, loss of community, and challenges of getting to work from far-off neighborhoods with little or no public transportation. If efforts to improve the public schools succeed, the town is likely to become an even greater magnet for higher-income residents, while lower- and middle-income residents will be forced to move out. In that event, Washington will be heading toward becoming a European-style town, where the better-off live downtown and the poor live in neighborhoods outside of town—the reverse arrangement of the typical American city of the second half of the twentieth century. Some writers have already foreseen this trend.

Further, Washington continues to face problems of deep poverty, with a fifth of its population, mostly black, living below the poverty line. Its crime rate is still too high. Its public schools remain very weak. It continues to suffer from some of the worst traffic congestion in the nation. It struggles with problems of air pollution from vehicle traffic and continuing pollution of its rivers from discharges upriver from the city and runoff from heavy rains that flow directly into the rivers. Finally, as the attack of September 11, 2001, demonstrated, Washington is a primary target for terrorists. Security concerns have resulted in several street closures and the erection of cumbersome barriers to entrances of government buildings. For several years after 9/11, the continuing sense of threat added an edge to life in the city and provoked many discussions at dinner tables of how to get out of the city in an emergency (it's not going to be easy with all the bridges) and where to go. It wouldn't take much to reignite that fear.

But for all of its problems, Washington has at last begun to approach the dreams that George Washington had for it and the plans that L'Enfant made for a city of nature, a city of symbolism and politics. But Washington has become known for more than its politics. It has also become a city of culture and intellectual endeavor. In short, it is a vibrant, diverse, lived-in city.

Politics in DC

National politics is the principal preoccupation of Washington, DC. But there is another realm of politics in Washington—that is, local politics. And the key political issue for Washingtonians since the creation of the city is who governs it. As mentioned earlier, the framers of the Constitution wrote that Congress "shall exercise exclusive Legislation in all Cases whatsoever" over the nation's capital. That provision has been interpreted to mean that Congress can review and overturn the laws and budgets of the city and that the city should have no voting representatives in either houses of the Congress. Washingtonians complain that they are living under "taxation without representation" and have put that complaint on their car license plates, T-shirts, and bumper stickers. The residents of the nation's capital are, in fact, the only American citizens without a vote in Congress, even though the city's population is larger than the population of Wyoming and Vermont.

The reason for this peculiar provision of the Constitution is that in 1783, when the Congress of the Confederation was sitting in Philadelphia, it was threatened by unruly mobs of unpaid Revolutionary War veterans, but the state of Pennsylvania refused to control them. Members of that Congress were forced to flee the city for a time. This incident, called the Philadelphia Mutiny, persuaded many at the later constitutional convention that the federal government must have

DMV

ultimate control of the nation's capital city to ensure the representatives' security as well as their dignity.

While Congress wanted control over the District of Columbia, it did not want to manage it directly. So as noted earlier, over the nearly 226 years of the city's existence, a variety of arrangements have been tried for municipal governance. The town started out with a mayor, who was appointed by the president, and a twelve-member council elected by property-owning white males who had resided in the city for at least a year. In 1820 citizens were allowed to elect their mayor as well—an early case of home rule. After the Civil War and during Reconstruction, black males (but not women of any race) were given the vote. In 1867 two blacks were elected to the city council; in 1870 seven blacks were elected to the council. The next year, Congress decided to abolish the existing government and combine Georgetown (still a separately governed town), Washington City, and Washington County (beyond the old city limits) into the District of Columbia. Congress determined it would be led by a governor and a council appointed by the president, with a nonvoting member of Congress. The political unification of the various pieces of DC made sense, but many also saw this change as a way of circumscribing the role of blacks in DC politics—and it effectively did. After Boss Shepherd grossly overspent on improvements to the city, Congress changed the city government again, creating spots for three commissioners appointed by the president to govern the city.

Nearly a century later in 1967, during the era of civil rights advocacy, Congress agreed to create a mayor/commissioner and a city council, both appointed by the president. In 1973, Congress turned these positions into elected ones. The era of home rule had begun, but the city still lacked a vote in either house of Congress, Congress still reviewed its laws and budgets, and the president still appointed its judges. And despite several efforts to persuade Congress to grant statehood to DC, it has not done so. Clearly, although the writers of the Constitution did, Congress no longer fears unruly demonstrators running them out of town. Resistance now comes from political inertia. So many other pressing issues face Congress and the president that granting statehood for Washington, DC—an effort that would require an amendment to the Constitution—is not important enough to garner the necessary votes.

Congress has also been concerned regarding the capacity of the DC government to manage itself effectively, a fear that was greatly exacerbated during Mayor Barry's four terms in office. This fear may be abating as more competent administrations have led the city in the years after 1998. Two other concerns have also likely played a role—a reluctance still on the part of some members of Congress and their constituents to empower what they feel would be a government (and new state) led by African Americans in the District of Columbia and a reluctance on the part of some Republicans to see another very strongly Democratic state (with its vote in the House and two votes in the Senate) added to Congress.

Washington is so liberal politically and so strongly oriented toward the Democratic Party that it is virtually a one-party district. The only competitive local elections are the primaries, where Democrats compete for the right to run in the general election. In general elections in DC, Republicans occasionally win a seat on the DC Council representing affluent areas of Northwest.

The reason for the Democratic Party's monopoly in Washington, DC, is in part based on its support from African Americans. The Democratic Party took the lead in passing civil rights laws in the 1960s and the Great Society programs to benefit the poor. The party's position on civil rights led to its loss of support from a generation or two of white Southerners that it had enjoyed since the Civil War, but the party solidified its support in the African American community. Added to the blacks' support for the Democratic Party in DC is the support it receives from the city's white liberals, who are typically well educated, politically aware, and socially progressive.

Proposals for full political rights and statehood for DC are unlikely to go away in the future regardless of the obstacles to their realization. Indeed, another proposal to gain political rights for the District is to retrocede to Maryland all of the city save the major federal buildings—the Capitol, the White House, and accompanying federal office buildings—and the Mall. For better or for worse, the state of Maryland has not shown much inclination to absorb DC. Truth be told, I believe Washingtonians would prefer to remain Washingtonians even if Maryland offered to do so.

There are other consequences, touched on earlier, of the peculiar political position of Washington, DC. Not only is much of the city's property, which is owned by the federal government, not part of the city's tax base, but also Congress has barred the city from enacting a tax on suburban commuters who travel there every day to work despite their use of city services and infrastructure. Thus, the city's tax base is considerably smaller than it would be if it were not a capital city. The federal government has provided an annual subsidy to the city's budget, but over the centuries, city officials and many residents have felt that subsidy is too small to cover both the city's needs and the city's costs—for example, in providing security to federal officials—given the federal government's presence.

Further, that the amount of the subsidy is decided by a body in which the city has no vote (and, thus, has a weak voice) has long rankled many Washingtonians. What also rankles are measures that Congress imposes on the city against the will of its residents: constructing multiple freeways (some of which, as we have seen, DC residents with great and prolonged effort successfully resisted), pushing for urban renewal in Southwest (residents were not consulted), insisting on a referendum on the death penalty in 1992 even though residents widely opposed the punishment (the referendum failed), and attempting to reverse local restrictions on gun ownership. Gun control is widely supported in the city. While Congress failed to reverse the laws, the Supreme Court ultimately declared the city's restrictions on gun ownership unconstitutional.

In the past, congressional rule of the District has meant neglect. Members of Congress, who see themselves as transients here, had little invested in the city, and their constituents had even less interest in its operations. Also, powerful segregationist Southern committee chairmen once exercised nearly unfettered control over the majority-black city. Washington, DC, today is much better organized politically to challenge unreasonable intrusions by Congress, and Congress at present seems unwilling to make too many of such intrusions. But the basic issues remain: Who really owns Washington, DC—its residents or the entire country? How can the political rights of its residents be protected while also safeguarding the interests of the federal government and the American people in their capital city? And, most basically, shouldn't Washingtonians in modern, democratic America have the same political rights that other Americans do, including having their own voting representatives in Congress?

Turning to the meat and potatoes of local politics, what are the other issues absorbing the city's interest, and which groups play a role in influencing them? The issues of Washington, DC, politics are not different from those of other major US cities: how to stimulate private investment and jobs while preserving historic properties in the city and how to provide effective services to residents and especially to the poor. These issues engage private developers, preservationists, and advocates for the poor. "Development" in Washington typically means private investment in housing, retail, hotels, sports facilities, entertainment, and small businesses.

The city has a number of ways of encouraging private developers—selling available land to them (often at below-market rates), making major public investments (for example, new Metro stations) in areas ready for development, and subsidizing loans and grants to developers—while requiring those developers to create infrastructure, low-income housing, and other amenities as part of their development contracts. The city can also seize land from private owners (with compensation) for development and other purposes, but using the power of eminent domain acquired a bad name after it was implemented to clear much of Southwest for redevelopment in the 1960s.

Laws and procedures (and watchful citizens) concerned with historic preservation also now constrain free-for-all development. Washington has forty-five official historic districts, mostly in the downtown and close-in areas. Various boards must review and approve changes in the districts' existing structures and open spaces to conserve their aesthetic, cultural, and historic qualities, thus providing a degree of protection against the destruction of buildings and neighborhoods that was all too common in the past.

The political tug of war that never ends is between promoting development and providing assistance for the city's poor. In the best of worlds, development can help the poor by creating jobs, neighborhood improvements, and larger tax revenues for the city government. But inevitably, public monies (subsidies, grants, access to land, and so on) for developers can leave less funding available for low-income housing, special education, health care, and other programs to help the city's poorest residents. These trade-offs are behind many political debates and tensions in the city. And ironically, development in poverty-stricken neighborhoods can hurt its needy residents by raising real estate prices and taxes, forcing them to relocate.

Finally, politics also affects the quality of city services— above all, public education. The city's public schools, like other services, were struggling before 1973 when the home rule era began. There seemed never to be enough money to fund all the services required, and they often suffered from neglectful management. The quality of the schools and other services deteriorated further during the first two decades of home rule when many appointments were based on patronage without effective oversight. By the beginning of the twenty-first century, Washington was spending more on average on children in public schools and getting the worst outcomes of any city in the United States. Repeated attempts to improve the school system ran aground in the face of bureaucratic complexities and resistance, fears on the part of school administrators and teachers' unions of politicizing hiring and firing policies, and the absence of sustained reform efforts over time. Being subject to the whims of Congress also affects education in Washington, with policies advocated by both the right and the left being implemented by turns. Former Speaker of the House John Boehner, a Republican, aggressively pursued the increased opportunity for establishing charter schools in Washington. Some of them have been successful, though many people still oppose their existence. At the time of this writing, another forceful effort to reform the schools is under way; the outcome is still unclear.

Crime also remains a concern, and as noted earlier, the amount of crime in DC dropped during the first decade of this century as it did in many US cities. But there remains enough street crime, shootings by youngsters of other youngsters, and gang-related violence to leave DC residents wary of wandering around on the streets late at night.

Many city services have been reformed, but corruption (in some cases, massive) and mismanagement remain problems in city government. Investigative journalists have become major sources of accountability where city management is concerned by uncovering one after another stories of egregious deficiency and scandal in city government. Problems of accountability surely have some of their source in the nature of DC politics; with one political party enjoying so much local support, the necessary political competition that usually forces governments to perform well is weak. Such is often the consequence of one-party states, whether local or national. Congressional interference in city decisions can further reduce accountability.

What interests and groups play a role in local Washington politics? In the early years of home rule, political power in DC's African American community shifted from traditional elites (in the person of the first mayor, Walter Washington) to younger, former civil rights and poverty activists led by Marion Barry, who was mayor for four terms. Barry then managed to create a supportive coalition of business interests (then mostly white), black churches (influential in much of the black community), unions, and white liberals. By the end of his third term (after which he went to jail for cocaine use), most of this wide-ranging support had withered away, but he remained popular among working-class and poor blacks, who reelected him once more after he was freed. The former mayor sat on the city council, representing one of the poorest wards in the city, till his dying day.

Because the city lacks a manufacturing sector and the unskilled jobs that typically accompany it, Washington never attracted the large number of immigrants from abroad that New York, Boston, and Chicago did. Neither did the strong industrial unions common in northern manufacturing towns develop in Washington, although it is worth noting that public sector unions for teachers, bus drivers, and others have flourished. Still, the lack of an overwhelming unionization of the workforce meant that politicians could run true grassroots campaigns and win. The sixth mayor, Adrian Fenty, did so in 2006, engaging in door-to-door "retail" politics and collecting small contributions from many individuals to win the election. (Once he had won the primary, the developers, law firms, and other sources of big money began to contribute to his campaign since it was clear he would be elected mayor.)

The role of ethnic politics at least seems set to change as the size of the Hispanic community as a percentage of DC citizens continues to grow. Should this community, which is made up primarily of immigrants from Central American countries and Mexico, coalesce into a coherent political force in the city, it could play an important role in local politics. Indeed, in the future, it could become a political king maker between a declining African American population and an increasing white population.

CHAPTER

3

Natural Washington

L ET US BEGIN our depiction of contemporary Washington
with the most basic characteristic of any city, its natural
environment. There is no other major city in the world where
nature is more present. Besides the broad grassy spaces of the
Mall, many parks and small triangles and circles of green
appear suddenly at the intersection of radiating avenues and
traffic circles. Almost all city streets—both close in and far
out—are bordered with trees, so much so that the houses in
the neighborhoods are hard to see from the air when the
leaves are out. Added to the mature trees, many houses and
apartments are surrounded by flowering bushes that erupt in
color in the spring. A major forest, Rock Creek Park, slices
through the northwest section of the city, creating a stretch of
wilderness in the middle of the busy urban environment.
Indeed, there is ample wildlife. For example, deer are in such
great supply in the city's parks and forests that they regularly
dine on nearby householders' flowers and devastate vegetable
gardens, leap across major avenues in the middle of traffic,
fall into the Tidal Basin (and have to be fished out), and even

wander into shops in Georgetown. Most recently, coyotes have begun to move into the city's wild areas and nearby suburbs, joining foxes, skunks, raccoons, and a vast number of squirrels.

Birds are especially numerous in Washington. Even in the close-in residential areas like Dupont Circle, the sounds of birdsong in the early mornings during spring can overcome the background hum of traffic and the din of airplanes. In the fall and spring, formations of geese frequently honk their way across the sky, reminding us that Washington was once a major stop for migrating waterbirds. Fireflies blink on and off in the dusk in the spring and summer. On fall evenings, the chirping of crickets seems just as loud as it does in the countryside outside the city. And during the warmer months throughout the town, there is the ever-present, mournful cooing of doves, a familiar part of the natural world of the American South in which Washington is geographically situated.

Another visible aspect of nature in Washington is the sky. With the many open parks, wide avenues, and height limits on buildings—in contrast to cities with skyscrapers—the view of the sky is pervasive. Adding to the presence of nature in the capital are the two major defining rivers, the Potomac and Anacostia (even if commuters grumble when they are stalled in rush hour traffic on the city's bridges).

It is often alleged that Washington is built on a swamp; however, that belief is not true. At the time of George Washington, the banks of the Potomac and Anacostia Rivers were firm, often with bluffs rising above the rivers and a few tidal marshlands along the rivers' edges. Numerous streams and creeks were within the area of the city, and during heavy rains or exceptionally high tides, the streams could breach their banks. These creeks now flow through pipes below the city streets. The largest one, the old Tiber Creek, flows beneath Constitution Avenue and still occasionally floods the basements of federal buildings there.

From the building of the city in the late eighteenth century, construction works in Washington and intensifying agriculture upstream created silt and mud deposits along the shores of the Potomac and Anacostia that may have eventually created so-called swamps. But in the words of a National Park Service study, Washington, at the time of the city's establishment, "was an attractive basin of river meadows and tidal marshes ringed by an amphitheater of hills, and not the fetid swamp so often described in today's popular histories and tourist literature."

The Bedrock of Washington: A Geologically Bifurcated City

Washington, DC, straddles two distinct geological zones—the Atlantic Coastal Plain that runs from New Jersey to Florida and the Piedmont Plateau that rises to the west toward the Appalachian Mountains. The White House, the Washington Monument, the Mall, and the close-in business and residential districts are part of a fan-shaped, relatively flat area of gravel deposits that is part of the coastal plain. The Capitol sits atop one of the hills looking over that plain.

Just north of the downtown area, the Piedmont Plateau, also called the Fall Line, rises by roughly two hundred feet. The beginning of this rocky plateau is visible as north–south streets suddenly start to climb about twenty blocks north of the White House. Even the weather is different above the Fall Line. It is somewhat cooler in the summer, and in the winter, snow can be falling at the top of the Fall Line while it is raining lower down in the city.

It was not an accident that Washington was built atop these two geological formations. The Fall Line marks the farthest point inland that ships can sail up the Potomac. Above the line are impassable rapids. The port of Georgetown (which was established in the mid-1700s, well before the founding of Washington, DC) was located at the farthest point inland of the navigable Potomac River.

A Town of Rivers

Two rivers and one major creek are currently part of the city (with the old Tiber Creek now underground and out of sight). The Potomac flows along the city's western border and is joined first by Rock Creek below Georgetown and then later by the Anacostia River. The Potomac River rises in the highlands of West Virginia, flowing north through the Cumberland Gap. It then turns south to wind its way around wooded islands, over gentle rapids, and past farmland and forest. At Harpers Ferry it leaves the mountains to join the two forks of the Shenandoah River and then heads fifty miles south toward

Washington. Several miles above the city, the river turns wild as it enters a narrow gorge to tumble seventy-five feet in a half mile over the rocks and through the twisted channels of Great Falls and Little Falls. Then, right above Georgetown, as the river reaches sea level, it calms and widens and begins a stately flow to the Chesapeake Bay, some hundred miles to the south, and to the Atlantic Ocean beyond.

The Potomac River is a third of a mile wide as it passes the Lincoln Memorial and expands to a mile wide just below the city, making it a much broader body of water than rivers that flow through other major world cities, such as the Thames in London, the Seine in Paris, or the Tiber in Rome. The Potomac has a major presence in Washington as a place for boating, crew races, and canoeing and as a backdrop for parks and national memorials. Theodore Roosevelt Island, just opposite the Kennedy Center, is a natural setting for walks with its many woods and paths. It was called Analostan Island after its Native American inhabitants and was later owned and occupied by the family of George Mason, a delegate to the Constitutional Convention who helped James Madison draft the Bill of Rights. The island is now a wooded nature preserve.

The Potomac River, for all of its considerable attractions, is not all that it could be. Indeed, it is still troubled by chemical leakage from old mines, silt and agricultural runoff from upriver, sewage overflows from Washington, and the intrusion of alien species of fish and plants. It is much cleaner today than it was in the 1970s, and the numbers of fish are growing again. But since the early 1920s, when there was a public beach near the Tidal Basin, the river has not been reliably clean enough for casual swimmers. I always hoped that someday I would be able to swim at a Tidal Basin beach as my mother did as a child in the early 1900s.

The Anacostia River flows into the Potomac at Haines Point. This river was once deep and protected enough to be a port for ocean-going sailing vessels. But it has long been neglected, and despite the heroic efforts of a number of citizen groups, it is silted up and dirty. It has great potential eventually to add to the city's charm as a river town. New sports, housing, and shopping areas plus riverside parks are planned for the Anacostia, but their realization appears to lie sometime in the future.

The Seasons of the Capital

Washington has a mid-Atlantic climate. Its summers are hot and humid like much of the American South, and its winters can be cold, reminiscent of more northern states. The seasons are thus very distinctive. And because nature has such a pervasive presence in Washington, the different seasons are very much a part of the yearly experience of life in the nation's capital.

I am always surprised to read that Washington's climate is considered subtropical. The city is in the temperate zone; how did the tropics sneak in? During the summer months, at least, it is too true that the heat sometimes approaches 100 degrees Fahrenheit (or nearly 40 degrees Celsius), and the percentage of humidity runs not far behind. Both are part of a common weather system that affects the region when cool, high-pressure air carried by the jet stream across Canada retreats north, permitting warm and humid air from the Gulf of Mexico to move in. The heat is made worse by two factors—the partial geographical bowl in which the center of the city is situated and the many buildings that hold and radiate heat. There is some relief to be had by fleeing the center to the hills around the city, but not much. Most people simply close up their houses, offices, and cars; crank up the air-conditioning; and pull down the window blinds. Before air-conditioning, all of those people who could do so escaped the city during July and August, and those left behind spent a great deal of time sitting on their front porches. At night some slept in the alleys outside or even drove to Rock Creek Park, where the air was fresher, and slept in their cars.

The evenings are long in the summer, with the light finally fading after 9 p.m. during July and August. These evenings give people plenty of time to participate in sports teams (each government office, congressional delegation, and private enterprise seems to have one) and play softball, volleyball, soccer, and more on the Mall and in and around the city. Then they take in a few beers or dinner afterward at one of the city's many street cafés.

Not all of summer is burdened with oppressive heat. There are sparkling days when the humidity drops, the temperature dips, and the sunlight is so bright that it hurts the eyes. Then there are days when the sky darkens in the west, thunderstorms burst on the city, and news forecasters warn of tornadoes. Also in late summer are times when high, breezy winds and low, rapidly circling clouds announce an approaching hurricane, and later heavy rain and wind bend and uproot trees, flood basements, and disrupt electricity.

If summer in Washington is infamous, the worst of it only lasts for two months, if that. The city experiences three other distinct seasons. Fall is a gentle time. The heat gives way to cool nights and warm days, and the humidity lessens. Mornings are often graced with mists that burn off as the sun rises. Leaves begin to turn yellow, orange, red, and brown. They seldom approach the glory of a New England autumn, but their colors are nonetheless striking. As leaves fall and accumulate on the streets and sidewalks and crinkle underfoot, the scent of their decaying suggests the declining year and the approaching winter.

Winter in Washington is now usually mild. It wasn't always that way. The mid-1900s saw days and weeks of bitter cold beginning in November. And even earlier in the twentieth century, the Potomac River often froze so hard that people could walk across it. Now winter is confined largely to January and February, with a few cold days in December and maybe a first frost in the city in mid-November. Street cafés often remain open in November and even December, and they are quick to reopen on warm days in March.

Snow, when it does come, usually falls in January or February. In recent years, with global warming, snow and ice have become rare. But every decade or so, a great blizzard hits that proves beautiful and exciting for children of all ages and a major headache for city managers who are then frequently overwhelmed with traffic accidents and snow-clogged streets they often cannot seem to clear. When even a dusting of snow creates traffic nightmares for Washingtonians, a real snowstorm with a foot or more of snow can paralyze the city for days. Schools and universities cancel classes, and city and federal government offices shut down because employees simply cannot reach them. At such times, Chicagoans and other people from northern states who hold prominent positions in DC take on airs about their superior abilities to deal with snow.

But a major snowfall, for all its problems, turns the capital into a magical place. The streets empty of people and cars, and the drone of airplanes disappears. The snow dresses the many trees and parks in white, smooths the sharp lines of railings and vehicles, and creates a blanket of silence. For those living in the downtown area, the city is quiet and empty—suddenly theirs for a time.

Darkness comes early in winter, even before offices empty for the evening. But for those in government buildings near the city's parks and memorials, there are special moments of beauty as the sun sets over the Potomac and the softening light bathes the Washington Monument and the Lincoln Memorial in pastels of pink and blue. I once worked in an office near the Mall and was often transfixed by the view on early winter evenings.

Just as winter becomes too tedious to endure any longer, spring in Washington begins slowly to unfold. Its first signs are often fearless little crocuses that pop up in front yards as early as February. They often meet their end quickly if there

A 2009 winter storm blankets the city.
Architect of the Capitol

is a cold snap. But they are soon followed by daffodils, which are more resistant to the cold, and then the luminous yellow flowers of forsythia bushes. By late March, the city's trees begin to put out delicate green leaves that obscure their spiky shadows in the wan, late-winter light.

By the beginning of April, flowering trees are in bloom: star magnolias, redbuds, dogwoods, and, above all, cherry trees. More than thirty-seven hundred cherry trees surrounding the Tidal Basin and other spots around the city's center create clouds of blossoms and draw crowds of visitors and Washingtonians to see them each spring and to participate in the Cherry Blossom Festival.

The Tidal Basin during cherry blossom season.
Eric Magnan

Many of these trees came from Japan as a gift from the city of Tokyo to Washington. Unfortunately the first shipment of two thousand cherry trees in 1910 had to be destroyed because they were infested with insects and nematodes. A second shipment of more than three thousand trees, taken from a special grove of cherry trees along the banks of Tokyo's Arakawa River, arrived in 1912 and were planted around the Tidal Basin, on the White House grounds, and elsewhere in the city. They flourished, but vandals cut down several of them shortly after the bombing of Pearl Harbor in 1941, presumably an expression of anti-Japanese sentiment. Fortunately, it was the only instance of damage done to the trees during World War II.

Tokyo's original stock of the trees deteriorated from wartime neglect. In 1952 the Japanese requested assistance from Washington to help restore their trees, so the National Park Service sent cuttings from the Tidal Basin cherry trees to Japan for that purpose. Clearly, the original gift of the Japanese cherry trees has created a special karma between Washington and Tokyo and between Americans and Japanese who celebrate the trees so much each spring.

A collection of more than a hundred varieties of tulips, known as the Tulip Library, flowers each spring on the north side of the Tidal Basin. In a city of more than 650,000 inhabitants, the National Park Service plants nearly as many tulips in the city's public gardens as there are residents (give or take 100,000). Perhaps the tulip should replace the American Beauty rose as the city's flower. Surely a great many more tulips bloom at their peak than there are roses (and the former are much less trouble to care for).

By the end of April, azaleas and other flowering bushes are in raucous bloom. They seem to occupy the front yards of many houses outside the downtown area, all the way to the distant suburbs. A whole park, the National Arboretum, is given over to ten thousand azalea bushes that flower at the end of April in what can only be called an orgy of color.

All of these flowers and trees, however, produce prodigious amounts of pollen. By late April, cars and other outdoor surfaces are usually covered with a yellow film. Those people with allergies then pop antihistamines between sneezing and rubbing itchy eyes. Allergies probably strike much of the population of Washington, for it is said that if you don't have them when you move to the city, you will get them soon enough.

By mid-May, the days are lengthening, and the city is once more dressed in the early exuberance of summer with masses of leafy trees, bright flower beds, and rapidly growing lawns. By now, it is hard to recall the rigorously austere, brown-and-gray town of only two months before.

Trees and Wildlife

At the end of the nineteenth century, Washington was known as the City of Trees. After nearly a century of neglect, in the 1870s, the city had finally built a sewage system, graded and paved streets and sidewalks, and planted trees. Many were American elms, surely one of nature's most elegant trees. The branches of the elm, where they have space, grow outward, arching over avenues and seemingly stretching out and over to embrace as large a space as possible.

Elms are Washington's heroic trees, fighting against Dutch elm disease but, increasingly, succumbing. Other heroic trees in the city are the two enormous tulip poplars in Montrose Park whose girth would require several people with outstretched arms to encircle them. My personal favorite is an enormous white ash on the campus of Georgetown University. Its branches extend horizontally in all directions, giving shade to students reading below, and its large and round crown is all encompassing.

One very special kind of tree, the witness tree, existed during a major historic event or during the life of a great, long-deceased person and lives to this day. Such trees are found in two places in Washington. President Andrew Jackson in 1829 planted two southern magnolia witness trees on the White House lawn that are still thriving, and an estimated ten witness trees on the grounds of Mount Vernon were planted at the time George Washington was living there, giving visitors a rare living tie to our first president.

We have already described some of the wildlife in Washington that finds refuge in the city's parks and wooded areas (and backyards), but one important species has not yet been mentioned—American bald eagles, the symbolic bird of America. Bald eagles had long made their homes in the region, especially along the Potomac River. They were almost wiped out in the 1950s as a result of using the chemical DDT to kill malaria-carrying mosquitoes. Since the chemical was banned in 1972, the eagle population has rebounded, and they have gradually returned to the area.

One pair in particular became national news. In the early years of the twenty-first century, George and Martha, a nesting pair of eagles, raised successive families of fledglings near the Wilson Bridge at the southernmost tip of the city. This pair was a particular source of delight—indeed, almost regarded as a special blessing—by Washingtonians as they showed that wildlife could recover in the wake of human depredations and, perhaps symbolically, that America itself could recover from its trials of the second half of the twentieth century. However, Martha and George had their downs as well as their ups. In 2006 another female attacked and badly wounded Martha, presumably intending to replace her in George's affections. Martha was sent to an animal rescue center in Delaware, where she recovered. She returned to rejoin George. Later, she collided with a power line and was so badly wounded that she was put to sleep. But another female soon appeared to pair with George. Undoubtedly many Washingtonians saw this story as a metaphor for much of the goings-on in the city but with an ending as happy as could be expected under the circumstances. At least the eagles were back.

Rock Creek and Other Parks

Rock Creek Park makes Washington, DC, unusual in the panoply of the world's capital cities. Few other national capitals have such a large area of forest within its boundaries, though Paris comes close with the more landscaped Bois de Boulogne.

Rock Creek Park is a long, narrow, and wooded river valley that begins north of the city and wends its way down to the Potomac River just below Georgetown. The idea to set Rock Creek aside as a park in Washington arose from President Lincoln's unhappiness with the unhealthy conditions surrounding the White House. Rapid silting had made the Washington Canal, which ran behind the White House, ugly, smelly, and unsanitary, especially in the heat of Washington summers. Understandably, President Lincoln and Mrs. Lincoln regularly abandoned the White House each summer evening for the Soldiers' Home seven miles to the north and spent the nights in a cooler and more wholesome environment.

As a result, a search was begun for a healthier place to locate the White House. Out of this effort came a proposal not to move the White House but to create an urban park out of what was then a place of natural beauty gradually being taken over by private real estate upstream and the dumping of garbage and the emptying of sewage downstream. Beginning in 1867, legislation was introduced in Congress to create Rock Creek Park and purchase the land within its boundaries. But for more than two decades, Congress failed to act. Members were reluctant to appropriate the needed funds, much as they were unwilling to spend funds generally for making improvements in the city at the time.

Finally, after decades of lobbying by the city's citizens, in 1890 Congress passed legislation that authorized the creation of Rock Creek Park (at the same time it created a national park system for the United States). It then took several years and a series of court decisions for the government to condemn and purchase the private property within the planned park's boundaries. In 1897 work began to improve the roads within the park but only because a chain gang of prisoners was available; Congress had neglected to appropriate funds to finance park improvements.

The park now contains not only a large forested area but also the National Zoo, picnic areas, an amphitheater, hiking and biking paths, horseback riding trails (and stables where horses can be rented), a golf course, and several roads for traffic through the park. A proposal in the 1960s to construct a multilane freeway through the park to carry commuters into the city was mercifully fended off, but the park still sees plenty of traffic during rush hour.

Similarly, the old Chesapeake and Ohio Canal and adjoining towpath that run from Georgetown to Cumberland, Maryland, have also been preserved as a national park where people can hike and bike. Other in-town trails for bikers and hikers through parks and wooded areas include the seven-mile Capital Crescent Trail, an old rail right-of-way with no streets to cross from Georgetown to Silver Spring. Just outside the city are two trails—the Sligo Creek Trail along another river valley that leads down to the Anacostia River, and the Mount Vernon Trail, which runs from the city to the first president's home in Virginia. Not far away is the multiuse W&OD Trail, which is built on the roadbed of the former Washington and Old Dominion Railroad and runs nearly fifty miles through Northern Virginia. Washingtonians have no excuses for not enjoying the outdoors.

After more than two hundred years and despite the pressures of wars and development, Washington today remains an environment created by man but pervaded by nature. Nature's bounty can be enjoyed even while it reminds Washingtonians of humanity's small place in an immense and miraculous universe.

CHAPTER

4

Cityscape

Pierre Charles L'Enfant is buried high up in Arlington National Cemetery in a quiet and peaceful spot overlooking Washington, DC. If he were able to see Washington today from that vantage point, he would look down across the Potomac River to the city he designed. In the distance, he would recognize the Capitol on the pedestal of land he planned for it. Looking through a telescope, he would wonder why the *Statue of Freedom* on the top of its dome was facing east since the city developed toward the west. The reason is symbolic: The sun should never set on freedom's face.

L'Enfant would surely be impressed by Washington's size and grandeur today. He would identify the Mall and recognize the White House a little to the left. In the foreground, he would see the tall, austere obelisk that is the Washington Monument. L'Enfant would have to guess what it is since the equestrian statue of George Washington he had planned was nothing like the monument of today. He might be surprised and curious about the Lincoln and Jefferson Memorials, which

The grave of Pierre Charles L'Enfant.
Eric Magnan

were not in his plan. Of course, Jefferson was yet to become president and Lincoln was not yet born when L'Enfant was planning the city. But L'Enfant probably would approve of the memorials as symbols of the country's great leaders.

Beyond this ceremonial core, L'Enfant would likely be heartened by the number of office buildings and residences that make up the city and continue into the distance. What he could not have envisioned is the kind of city that has grown up behind what he created—an international city. He would be astonished to see a collection of museums with a variety of architectural styles framing the Mall instead of the embassies he had envisioned, but he would likely appreciate the quality of Washington's museum exhibits if he could visit them. And the Washington National Cathedral north of the Mall—plus a large number of interesting church towers and steeples in the distance and even a minaret from the large mosque in the city—was not built in his time either.

Pierre L'Enfant would undoubtedly recognize the city he planned. On the one hand, he would probably be pleased with its appearance and might even remark on how closely, nearly two centuries later, it resembles his grand vision. On the other hand, he would probably also be outraged at the ways in which his plan has been changed. (It reportedly did not take much to provoke his anger when someone tampered with his work.)

First of all, he might well be concerned about the proliferation of memorials on the Mall; if not controlled, they threaten to turn the nation's front yard into its attic. He might have found one of them, the National World War II Memorial with its fifty-six pillars, two arches, fountains, and plaza, an excessively busy interruption of the long view between the Washington Monument and the Lincoln Memorial and on to Virginia and the West. Second, given his graceful and dignified designs, he would surely be horrified by the plaza that bears his name just south of the Mall. With its eight massive commercial and government buildings and hotels, it is crossed by broad streets that have more cars than people but usually not many of either (the people are presumably in the underground mall or offices) and is bounded to the south by an elevated freeway.

He would surely be incensed by the placement of the Treasury Department as the building interrupts the direct view he had planned from the Capitol to the White House. Historical lore has it that after arsonists burned the Treasury Building in 1833, President Andrew Jackson, angry at Congress, decided to rebuild it on Pennsylvania Avenue so as to block his view of the Capitol. Neither would L'Enfant be amused by the tangle of freeways through Southeast and Southwest, interrupting the long vistas he had planned for his major avenues and, in effect, isolating the Jefferson Memorial. Undoubtedly much more in Washington today would irritate L'Enfant; it is, after all, a mature, lived-in city with all the clutter and improvisation that comes with more than two hundred years of expansion. Yet in the end, L'Enfant would almost certainly be heartened that his basic plan for the capital of what was then a new and ambitious experiment in democracy has survived, as well as that democracy itself.

Beyond the Ceremonial Core

Beyond the ceremonial core of the new capital, as noted previously, L'Enfant foresaw a city that combined a traditional street grid overlaid by grand avenues radiating from the Capitol and the White House. He anticipated the "downtown"—the area around the Capitol and along Pennsylvania Avenue—would be home to residences and businesses. He expected houses and shops to fill in the many blocks in the city.

While it took two centuries, the city L'Enfant envisioned after traipsing through the woods and old fields covering what is now Washington has taken shape. The downtown area of offices and stores has grown up in an arc from the Capitol west toward the White House and Georgetown and north along Connecticut Avenue toward Dupont Circle. Indeed, this area of residences, shops, and entertainment grew up in the first half of the twentieth century and then almost died between 1950 and 1990 with the flight of the middle class to the suburbs and the lingering aftermath of the 1968 riots. But since the 1990s, the city has changed with the expansion of the Metro and the opening sports arenas, a grand theater complex, many new shops, restaurants, and apartments that have extraordinarily revitalized its street life. Perhaps it is my imagination, but sometimes I think I can hear L'Enfant cheering that Washington, DC, has come back to life and is now as vibrant and exciting as any downtown in the United States.

Within the arc north of Pennsylvania Avenue is the main business district, which includes K Street, the well-known location of many lobbyists, think tanks, and prosperous law firms. With the phalanx of ten- to twelve-story concrete and glass structures along K Street and other downtown streets, the architecture of commercial Washington is not inspiring or imaginative, but neither is it repellent. Washington commercial architecture seems set to remain comfortably conservative, functional, . . . and a little boring. Legal limitations on the height of buildings in the city—no taller than the Capitol or the width of adjacent streets plus twenty feet—

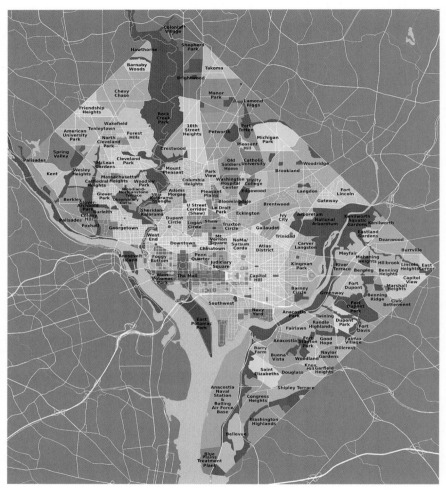

Neighborhoods of Washington, DC.

Peter Fitzgerald

have kept the skyline mercifully low but may have discouraged architectural variety.

Behind the business district are the in-town residential neighborhoods of nineteenth-century and early twentieth-century row houses. In these places, houses and corner shops mix with museums, parks, and shopping and entertainment areas. Despite the anonymity of city life, the residents of these neighborhoods often know one another and their local shopkeepers through frequent patronage of the shops, through walking their dogs, or through their participation in citizen organizations and neighborhood events such as block parties, street festivals, and local food and wine tastings. A number of neighborhoods, including Capitol Hill, Dupont Circle, and Georgetown, are now historic districts with restrictions on altering the existing buildings and cityscape. The restrictions in effect constrain redevelopment in the city and ensure that the greater downtown area is a lively, mixed-use one and not simply abandoned after the workday is done. We are currently seeing a growth in mixed-use communities throughout the city.

One of the largest in-town neighborhoods is Capitol Hill, home to many congressional staff, lawyers, and journalists. This area includes the Marine Barracks, where evening Taps is played in the summer; the Library of Congress; the Folger Shakespeare Library, with the largest collection of Shakespeare materials in the world; the Supreme Court; and the Capitol itself with its associated office buildings. At the end of the tree-lined, residential streets are often small grocery shops, and among the houses and streets are many little parks.

A residential street in Capitol Hill.
Eric Magnan

Many bars, cafés, restaurants, and bookshops line Pennsylvania Avenue. Nearby is the Eastern Market, the only nineteenth-century public market still operating in the city. Local residents can buy fresh farm produce and prepared food at the indoor stalls and items from the outdoor flea market.

To the northwest of the White House is Dupont Circle. Two great avenues frame part of this area—Connecticut Avenue, which angles northwest and has upscale offices and shops along it, and Massachusetts Avenue, which runs on an east–west diagonal through Dupont Circle and is crowded with think tanks and offices of major nongovernmental organizations. Massachusetts Avenue west of the circle is known as Embassy Row and is the site of many of the offices and residences of foreign delegations in the capital. Embassies of smaller countries are typically located in the splendid nineteenth-century mansions that newly rich industrialists and miners first built in this neighborhood when they decided to move into the city. To the north of Dupont Circle is a several-block-long area known as the Strivers' Section, which was an enclave of upper- and middle-class African Americans during the last decades of the nineteenth century and the first half of the twentieth century.

Dupont Circle is the most reminiscent of old European towns with its mix of residences. Victorian brick and stone row houses abound, some with small patios in the back, and

A residential street in Dupont Circle.
Eric Magnan

they blend easily with the area's modern apartment houses, cafés, galleries, museums, gyms, shops, and small theaters.

The Dupont Circle area attracts mainly professionals, a few families with children, and older empty nesters. It is also the center of much of Washington's gay life with an annual Capital Pride parade held every June. The popular Seventeenth Street High Heel Race takes place annually just before Halloween. Hundreds of men dress up as women, often very convincingly, and attired in high heels, they totter as quickly as they can several blocks to the finish line amid the cheering of thousands of spectators.

Moving west, across Rock Creek Park and all the way to Georgetown University, is the neighborhood of Georgetown. The oldest neighborhood in the city, it precedes the establishment of Washington by fifty years. This area is bordered by the Potomac River and bisected by two major commercial thoroughfares. To the south is M Street, with upscale shops, restaurants, banks, hotels, and bars. Running from the river to the north is Wisconsin Avenue, another busy commercial street built, it is said, on an old Indian path. Behind these busy avenues are quiet residential streets with a mix of small two-story and large three- or four-story row houses, often with their little side or back gardens.

To the east of Wisconsin Avenue, nearly every street has a church. Many of the churches used to serve the large and flourishing black community that once lived in this neighborhood, but that community has long since departed, with only a few aging congregants returning for Sunday services. The area also has four of the nicest parks in the city: Montrose

A street in Georgetown.
Eric Magnan

Park next to the old Oak Hill Cemetery sports some of Washington's oldest trees; Rose Park, a little-known area with sports fields, tennis courts, and children's climbing equipment, is tucked into the edge of Georgetown and Rock Creek Park; the Waterfront, at the base of Georgetown and the Potomac River, has restaurants, green space, and an outdoor recreation area; and the old Chesapeake and Ohio Canal has walking and biking paths along the Potomac River.

Georgetown, the most upscale in-town neighborhood of Washington, is known for the prominent politicians, journalists, lawyers, and hostesses who live there. To the chagrin of many residents, they must also contend with the noisy students who inhabit not only the campus of Georgetown University but a number of houses nearby as well. They also frequent M Street's restaurants and bars, which draw many other young people from all over town.

Besides these best-known and most vibrant in-town neighborhoods in Washington, there are others. For example, Shaw (east of Dupont Circle) and Logan Circle were once blighted and run down but now are in the process of revitalization. Columbia Heights (north of Shaw) is home to a lively Latin American community and is also rapidly undergoing renewal. The West End / Foggy Bottom area primarily consists of apartments and diplomatic institutions and is bisected by several major highways, thus it lacks much of a community, lived-in atmosphere. Penn Quarter, located north of Pennsylvania Avenue between the Capitol and the White House and near the Verizon Center, only a decade or so ago was dead in the evening with empty buildings and still suffered from the consequences of the riots and destruction of 1968. Now it is one of the hottest spots in downtown, especially for young people. And there is Southwest, formerly an area of dilapidated row houses and shops that were razed in the 1960s for redevelopment. This sector, which is in effect cut off from the rest of the city by the Southwest Freeway and the large office buildings south of the Mall, is still undergoing further development with the Nationals' baseball stadium and the massive reconstruction of its waterfront.

In-town Suburbs

Washington has many in-town suburbs, neighborhoods located mostly in the northern part of the city that had been summer retreats or farms during much of the nineteenth century. In the twentieth century, as public transportation expanded and the city's population grew, these areas filled in with new houses. The separation of residential areas from shopping areas that is so typical of the outer suburbs generally prevails in these neighborhoods too, where houses are mostly detached and have sizable yards in front and back. Stores and businesses are not usually within walking distance; rather, they are clustered on main streets such as upper Connecticut Avenue, Georgia Avenue, and Wisconsin Avenue.

Three of these neighborhoods are especially interesting for the different aspects of Washington they exhibit: Cleveland Park, an affluent area in the northwest quadrant of the city; Takoma Park in the city's upper northeast, spilling over into the Maryland suburbs next door; and Anacostia, a largely poor area but with an African American middle class in Southeast.

Cleveland Park, named after President Grover Cleveland who had a summer home there, is one of the wealthier close-in neighborhoods of the city, and many successful Washington professionals live in the community. Sandwiched between Wisconsin and Connecticut Avenues, the area features mostly genteel, single-family dwellings on quiet, tree-lined streets. Its many frame houses with wraparound porches are reminiscent of the kinds of summer homes built outside the downtown area in the nineteenth and early twentieth centuries. In some parts of Cleveland Park, residents can hear the tolling of the bells at the National Cathedral. Others can walk a short distance to the National Zoo.

In the upper northwest section of the city, Takoma Park bears some resemblance to Cleveland Park with its quiet, tree-lined streets and frame houses with wraparound porches and yards, but it has an even greater feel of being a village given its commercial area of mainly small shops. The neighborhood straddles the border between Washington and Maryland. Although not as affluent as the Cleveland Park neighborhood, Takoma Park in the nineteenth century was also a place where city residents sought clean air and cooler temperatures during the summers. Later in that century, it developed into a denser neighborhood for people who could use the train line passing through it to commute to work elsewhere in the city. From the beginning, the community was politically active. Residents created a citizens association in 1888 that, unlike most such associations at that time, admitted women as members; a historical society in 1912; and the Civic Study Club, which was later renamed the Takoma Park Women's Club, in 1913. The citizens association proceeded to lobby for recreational facilities, libraries, and other amenities.

Takoma Park today is a neighborhood of mostly middle-class professionals. It remains one of the most politically active neighborhoods in the Washington region. In the mid-twentieth century, the neighborhood was successfully integrated through the efforts of its residents (an unusual achievement given the tendency for whites then to flee a neighborhood as blacks moved in). When planners proposed building a spur of the Inner Loop freeway through the neighborhood, residents united successfully to block it, declaring, "No White men's roads through Black men's homes."

In 1983 the Maryland side of Takoma Park, now organized into a city with a mayor and town council, declared the city a nuclear-free zone, prohibiting the production of nuclear weapons there and, more to the point, preventing the city from investing in or purchasing or leasing goods or services produced by any enterprises that produce such weapons. The prohibitions are still in effect. The integrated, activist nature of Takoma Park gives it something of a "crunchy granola" reputation in the region.

Even before more affluent Washingtonians moved out of the downtown area to the northern sections of the city, working-class Washingtonians moved and settled on the south side of the Anacostia River. As noted previously, I lived near the banks of the Anacostia as a young child and grew up in Congress Heights near Saint Elizabeths Hospital. Blue-collar whites and blacks, many working across the river in the Navy Yard, lived in separate communities in what was then called Uniontown. It was the first neighborhood to be developed outside the old downtown area and later evolved to become Anacostia. Today, it is primarily an African American neighborhood of working- and middle-class homes and pockets of poverty. Like many poor urban areas, it lacks many amenities—coffee shops, restaurants, and entertainment—and endures a relatively high crime rate. Yet the neighborhood itself is a pleasant one with modest houses that have porches and lawns, with some spectacular views of the city, and with a potentially beautiful waterfront along the Anacostia River. It is also the site of Cedar Hill, the home of Frederick Douglass, the black abolitionist who was prominent in national and city life during the second half of the nineteenth century.

Anacostia appears to be on the brink of revitalization. It now has a Metro stop. Plans for developing the waterfront are under consideration, along with the possibility of increased public transportation options to link residents with the city. And plans for moving a large federal agency—the Department of Homeland Security—to the area are proceeding. In a promising sign that the area's revitalization has begun, data on real estate sales and increases in property values suggest that the demand for housing and housing prices have risen faster in and around Anacostia than in the rest of the city.

Beyond DC's Borders: The Metropolitan Area

The city of Washington is part of the large Washington metropolitan area, which includes the counties of Maryland, Virginia, and even West Virginia and extends from the Chesapeake Bay in the east to the Appalachian Mountains in the west and from the Pennsylvania border to the north to deep into southern Maryland in the south. This area, tied directly or indirectly to the economy of the city, has the seventh largest population in the United States with five million people, and ranks sixth as the fastest growing.

The population of the entire metropolitan area is 46 percent white, a little more than 25 percent black, 13 percent Hispanic, and 10 percent Asian. The end of the twentieth century and beginning of the twenty-first century saw a large inflow of immigrants, both professional and working class, from a variety of countries, and a large proportion settled in the suburbs. For example, Eden Center, a Vietnamese shopping center in Northern Virginia, has 120 shops and restaurants serving many, many Vietnamese patrons. Numerous Indian restaurants and shops operate in Montgomery County in Maryland, just north of the city. Newspapers, radio and TV stations, shops, churches, restaurants, theaters, and other amenities serve a large and diverse community of immigrants from Latin America in the city and the close-in counties of Virginia and Maryland. All of these groups have their own newspapers, radio programs, and cultural organizations that host many events. In fact, in recent years a portion of the increase in population of the Washington metropolitan area has come from immigration.

When I studied abroad in Bolivia in the 1960s, I lived with a wonderful family who has since moved to Washington and thrived. They are part of the diverse immigrant community that is a crucial and often-overlooked part of the makeup of Washington's society. Connecting with these communities is something I have tried to do throughout my life. I love and have an aptitude for language. I mastered French well enough to give speeches in West Africa. I was also able to give interviews to Spanish-language networks on American politics. A glass of wine beforehand always helped me loosen up when trying to discuss complex policy in a language besides English. Being able to connect with people on their own terms is a great way to make friends and earn people's respect. Making this effort has served me well in the cosmopolitan mix of Washington. (My son even tells me that when I speak with my rural cousins, I often adopt a bit of a twang!)

Roughly 10 percent of the five million residents in Washington's suburbs commute to work in the city every day, some driving (on a good day) an hour and a half each way. On a bad day, a traffic jam can add an hour to the commute. The city itself is often unable to meet the financial burdens of maintaining transportation infrastructure owing to its small tax base relative to the amount of commuters coming in and out of the city daily. Worse, the city is especially vulnerable to major and prolonged traffic tie-ups from political demonstrations (sometimes by irate citizens who intentionally block traffic to call attention to their cause) and from the frequent but usually short street closures that police arrange for visiting dignitaries or when the president or vice president race around town. Washingtonians can identify the difference between the sirens of police cars protecting a motorcade and the sirens of police cars hurrying to respond to an emergency: A motorcade produces a flock of sirens, all wailing at the same time. A president's movements can also be perceived from the traffic overhead as police helicopters at times hover over the place where he is visiting.

As the population of the Washington metropolitan area continues to grow, questions arise about the limits of suburban and exurban expansion and whether workers will tolerate the long commutes these distances impose. As we have seen, congestion is not new to the city and its surroundings; indeed, the problem motivated the freeway enthusiasts in the 1960s to construct highways through urban neighborhoods. Civic associations and preservation groups, however, appear strong enough to block such proposals in the future. To ease gridlock, expanding the Metro system is one alternative actively under consideration; creating additional rapid rail is another. A third proposal involves raising the height limits on buildings outside the city center to accommodate a denser use of close-in areas—for example, near Metro stations. Providing easy access to rental cars and bikes is yet another popular option. And an increasing number of in-town Washingtonians walk to work every day. One survey shows that nearly 12 percent of the locals do so, second in the United States only to Boston. Washington and its environs are experimenting, like other urban areas, with how to transport residents and visitors comfortably and preserve the essential urban environment.

Washington's Architecture

Washington is a city of museums. It is also something of an architectural museum itself. The style of many of the buildings in its monumental core is classicism, according to the wishes of both George Washington and Thomas Jefferson, who sought to symbolize and legitimize the new republic by tying its major buildings to those of the ancient democracies of Greece and Rome. The columns; the Doric, Ionic, and other capitals; the pediments; the friezes; the arches and domes—typically dressed in pale marble, granite, and other stone—all are common on many government buildings and museums in the center of town. The Capitol is the largest of these structures. The Lincoln Memorial recalls the Acropolis in Athens (but the purity of its whiteness recalls the Taj Mahal), while the Jefferson Memorial suggests the Pantheon in Rome. The architect of Union Station reportedly had the Roman baths in mind. Along with the Supreme Court, the Library of Congress, and the West Building of the National Gallery of Art, the architecture of these buildings gives a certain coherence and formality to much of official Washington.

Critics of the classical impulse in Washington architecture complain that later buildings in that style became "progressively larger, more sterile and less graceful in conception and execution." This critique was directed especially at the stolid complex of government buildings in the Federal Triangle on the south side of Pennsylvania Avenue and at the massive Rayburn House Office Building, which Ada Louise Huxtable, the former architecture critic for the *New York Times*, described, with some justification, as exhibiting "elephantine aesthetic banality" and the "apotheosis of humdrum."

Not all of Washington's stately buildings fit the formal, classical model. And not all buildings are white, pink, or buff in color. The Smithsonian Castle on the Mall, constructed of red sandstone, stands out in contrast with its medieval towers and turrets. Next to the Castle is another museum, the Arts and Industries Building, of red brick with white trim and several of its own towers. An American Institute of Architects guide to Washington describes these two buildings as "feudal twins" that add an element of "Gothic horror" to relieve the formality of the Mall.

The National Museum of the American Indian adds a further architectural style to America's front yard. It is built of undulating courses of yellow limestone blocks (to represent sculpting by wind and water), with an outside garden and marsh containing local plants (much as its site was before the European intrusion). The building evokes a feeling of warmth and placidity and flows unlike any other structure on the Mall.

Just visible from the Mall is the White House, a building in the Georgian style and a version of classical architectural styles. Thomas Jefferson was said to have complained it was too large: "big enough for two emperors, one Pope, and the grand Lama." He would have had a different view today with the offices, formal reception rooms, and other public uses to which the house is now put. (Hillary Clinton, when she was First Lady, had a minuscule office on the second floor of the White House that was almost certainly a converted food pantry.) Although a graceful building on the outside, the tightness of the indoor space plus the heavy security surrounding the building and its grounds led President Bill Clinton, who did not like to be restrained, to grumble that it was "the crown jewel of the US penal system."

The occasional complaints about the White House and other treasured buildings in Washington point to an interesting aspect of Washington architecture. People roundly criticize many of the city's buildings when they are first constructed, but people come to love them over time. The most spectacular example of this conversion is the Eisenhower Executive Office Building—a massive, gray wedding cake structure with stacked terraces of nine hundred Doric columns all around it—that now houses a variety of councils and agencies reporting to the president.

When it was completed in 1875, historian Henry Adams called it an "architectural infant asylum," and others so criticized it that the architect committed suicide. President Herbert Hoover wanted to tear it down (he was stopped as there was no money to do it in the Depression). In 1958 President

The Eisenhower Executive Office Building.
Eric Magnan

Harry Truman declared, "But I don't want it torn down. I think it's the greatest monstrosity in America." It was not torn down and has surely found a place in the hearts of all Washingtonians who love their city's wayward structures despite (or because of) their outrageous but very entertaining peculiarities.

The Kennedy Center is also one of those buildings whose design distressed critics. One critic termed it a "glorified candy box," and locals have called it a shoebox. But many Washingtonians have become fond of it, even as isolated as it is by multiple freeways surrounding it, and it has become an icon of Washington culture. It seems in Washington as elsewhere that

The John F. Kennedy Center for the Performing Arts.
Eric Magnan

when residents begin applying nicknames to prominent buildings, it is a sign they love them.

Some Washington buildings, though, will never be loved. The Rayburn House Office Building, for instance, may end up in that category. And the building that is surely among least loved in the city is the J. Edgar Hoover Building on Pennsylvania Avenue that houses the Federal Bureau of Investigation (FBI). Its architectural style, appropriately, is known as Brutalism.

A massive, yellow-tinged structure of poured concrete and glass, the building looms over the avenue with a superstructure

The J. Edgar Hoover Building, viewed from
Pennsylvania Avenue and Tenth Street.
Eric Magnan

of top floors that further juts over the front of the building. It has no street-level shops and has been closed to the public since 1999 for security reasons. It's hard not to think it is ugly, menacing, and out of place. Efforts currently under way to move the FBI headquarters to a nearby suburb may finally usher in the building's demise.

For the many dull and unloved stone and glass boxes along K Street and elsewhere in the city's business districts, some relief appears to be on the way, at least for the commercial buildings. Increasing numbers of these structures are having their stone or concrete exteriors replaced by glass curtains;

The Newseum, which moved from nearby Rosslyn, Virginia, to Pennsylvania Avenue in 2008.
Eric Magnan

their entire facades are enveloped with glass, imparting a welcome lightness to these areas. An example of a glass curtain wall is seen in the Newseum (a museum for news), a few blocks east from the FBI Building on Pennsylvania Avenue.

Among the most loved structures in Washington are three: the East Building of the National Gallery of Art, designed by I. M. Pei; the Vietnam Veterans Memorial, designed by Maya Lin; and the Metro (or, as most Americans call it, the subway). Commonly known as the East Wing, the East Building of the National Gallery is a triangular-shaped modernist building faced with pink marble that fits remarkably well in the wedge-shaped space it occupies and into the classical building design common to the monumental core of the city. The Vietnam Veterans Memorial on the Mall includes the V-shaped memorial wall of polished black granite that is sunk into the ground with the names of 58,307 (as of May 2015) American dead and missing etched into it. It is a place of solemnity and reflection where visitors often touch the names of relatives and friends and leave mementos on the ground beneath the names. The wall seems to express well the poignancy and sorrow and loss that accompanied that war for so many people.

The DC Metro and its stations are popular, despite frequent safety problems and increasingly crowded platforms and cars, not only because it eases travel in DC but also because of the spaciousness, simplicity, and cleanliness of its stations. They are all built primarily with concrete in a common, modernist style with hints of classicism that includes high, arched ceilings and coffered groins (repeated recessed panels on the walls and ceilings of the stations) that hold indirect lighting. The

Metro Center station.
Eric Magnan

forty-year-old system is, however, showing its age, and efforts are under way to make needed repairs to its infrastructure.

A note needs to be taken of Washington's "compromise architecture," presumably appropriate to building in a democracy. The historic preservation movement is influential in Washington and has done a great deal to protect many valuable buildings from being torn down and neighborhoods from being destroyed. But pressures downtown from the federal government, developers, and business groups for more office space have resulted in a peculiar compromise between preservationists and developers. The facades and at times the interiors of original buildings (usually old houses of three or four stories) are preserved while large ten- or twelve-story buildings are constructed behind them. Critics have called this practice, evident in Lafayette Square across from the White House and on Pennsylvania and Twenty-First Street, "facadomy." It often does not work artistically since the taller buildings tower over and overwhelm the preserved facades, and the whole point of preservation is lost. Sometimes, democratic politics and quality architecture simply do not mix.

We have already examined some of the close-in neighborhoods in Washington, but it is worth further noting that these neighborhoods have their own architectural styles as well. Georgetown, the oldest of all the neighborhoods in Washington, is a place of Federalist architecture with a dash of Victorian. The restrained, classical facades of many houses in Georgetown (with enough variety within this style)—plus the little corner shops (for wine, groceries, antiques) tucked in and the numerous churches—give the neighborhood a rhythm and coherence that make strolling a pleasure for any flaneur in the area. Capitol Hill offers the wanderer the opportunity to admire architecture of Victorian inspiration, with streets upon streets of corner shops and two-story houses with bay fronts. Dupont Circle is another neighborhood of two- and three-story red-and-brown brick Victorian row houses—many with conical roofs, towers, and other amusing conceits. The Victorians are interrupted by larger apartment buildings (but not so much as to lose the architectural coherence of the neighborhood).

A word also needs to be said about religious architecture in Washington. Pierre L'Enfant planned for a national church, but given the sensitivities regarding the separation between church and state in the new republic, no one ever built such a church. Instead, the city became the site of many hundreds of churches plus synagogues, mosques, Buddhist shrines, Hindu temples, and other places of worship and religious schooling. Two churches in particular stand out for their architectural styles: the National Cathedral, the seat of the bishop of the Episcopal Church, stands on Mount St. Alban, overlooking much of the city; and the Basilica of the Shrine of the Immaculate Conception next to the Catholic University of America in Northeast.

The National Cathedral is a Gothic structure, reminiscent of ancient English cathedrals except that its limestone walls are buff in color, unstained by time. It has a vaulting roof, arches and stone carvings inside, and flying buttresses outside and is graced with two hundred brilliant stained-glass windows—some of very modern design. The first stone was laid in 1907, and with the construction of the west towers eighty-three years later, it was finally completed. The cathedral is as close to a national church as Washington is likely to get. It has been the site of funeral services for many presidents and other prominent Americans and is the place where prayers are said for a new president the day after the inauguration.

The Basilica of the Shrine of the Immaculate Conception, opened in 1959, is the largest Catholic church in North America. Its style is Romanesque-Byzantine, reminiscent of the great churches of the eastern Mediterranean with its massive size and large dome of colored tiles. One of the reasons the planners of this basilica did not give in to the Gothic temptation is that the National Cathedral was already under construction as a major Gothic church in Washington.

Finally, the architecture of the embassies is noteworthy. Foreign governments often like to showcase themselves with embassies, both residences and office complexes, that symbolize their country. Governments of major countries frequently elect to build their own embassies. The British embassy looks for all the world like the country seat of a great duke or earl. While the French ambassador's residence—an old, stately home that is separate from the offices of the embassy—is similar to a chateau, the embassy's offices are in a seemingly small, gated French colony with, significantly, a plaque in the reception room honoring Pierre L'Enfant. Germany's embassy is big and modern and square, resembling the parts of Berlin that were recently rebuilt after the fall of the Berlin Wall and the reunification of the city. The Japanese ambassador's residence is also big and modern but with a touch of Zen, an inspiration that conveys the sense of nature, simplicity, and balance so characteristic of much Japanese design. The Russians have built an embassy with what can only be described as a vast Soviet style. One of the most delightful embassies is that of Sweden. Built on the Potomac riverfront not far from the Kennedy Center, it is very Nordic and modern with an openness and light from an interplay of water, glass, and wood. At dusk, when it is lit up, it can appear as a crystal floating in the evening air.

With all the brilliant variety of architecture in Washington, much of it is imitative of styles developed long ago and far away. Little of it could be called adventurous or original, undoubtedly reflecting the political nature of the city where one neither takes too many chances, publicly at least, nor acts too obviously eccentric. However, it almost happened that a very modern, adventuresome building was constructed for the former Corcoran Gallery of Art, once the largest private cultural institution in the city. The gallery, both an exhibition hall and a teaching facility, was housed in a building of classical inspiration near the White House. Its administration decided to expand its space by building a new wing and hired Frank Gehry, an internationally recognized architect, to design it. His design was daring for Washington—a series of large, undulating metallic sheets folded over one another that would cover the entrance to the new facility. The Fine Arts Commission approved the design, but a shortage of funding led the Corcoran board to cancel the project. This was a pity since the new wing, albeit undoubtedly edgy and controversial, would have likely become iconic quickly and have fallen into the category of outrageous (for DC) but loved buildings. No doubt it would have acquired an endearing local nickname, too. And it may have set a precedent for more audacious architecture in the city. (Instead, it was a harbinger of tougher times to come. The Corcoran dissolved in 2014, with the building and college going to George Washington University and the art collection going to the National Gallery of Art.)

Commerce

One of the questions I always ask about any city is, what makes its economy run? In Washington, DC, the major source of economic activity is the federal government. It employs a third of the workforce and produces a third of the gross domestic product in the city. Indirectly—because the federal government has increasingly outsourced a great deal of what it does to the private sector—its role in the local economy is much larger. It contracts for a wide range of services, including consulting, project management, research, and so much else.

The impact of government contracting can be seen in numerous aspects of the local economic scene. First, over the past decade and a half, it has helped fuel the rapid growth in the "professional and technical services" sector both within the city and in the surrounding suburbs. This expansion in what many call a knowledge economy results in the Washington metro area's employees being among the highest paid on average in the United States.

A second effect of the federal presence is that despite economic downturns, the continuity in government expenditures provides a degree of stability to the local employment market as well as to the real estate market, entertainment, retail establishments, and restaurants in the city. Another indirect consequence of the federal government's work in Washington is the boost it gives to employment for law firms (practicing before the federal bench as well as advising clients with legal and policy issues involving government issues), consultants, think tanks, public relations firms, public and private interest associations, and the city's many lobbyists. Finally the federal government uses set-asides for minority-owned firms that are designed to increase economic equity for African Americans and have undoubtedly helped to raise the percentage of black-owned businesses in Washington to a quarter of the total, far larger than the national percentage. This policy has come under attack, however, as gentrification has changed the composition of the city.

None of these facts is surprising. The federal government has long been the city's economic engine. More interesting is a trend toward greater private sector investment and employment in the city and in the region. As of 2014, thirty Fortune 1000 companies were headquartered in Washington, DC. These concerns included utilities, media, banking and finance, computer and information technologies, defense and security equipment, hotels, and publishing. Not all of them were reliant on government expenditures and contracts. And the hope is for those companies that do rely on government contracts—for example, those in information technologies or biological and health-related research—that they might become a source of strength in their own right and a major focus of economic activity independent of the federal government.

In short, while Washington is still a long way from becoming the great commercial center that George Washington envisioned, it is diversifying economically, adding to the city's and the region's wealth and, moreover, to the wealth and variety of its population and society. Meanwhile, with the strong and expanding federal presence and expenditures, inevitable economic downturns in the US economy may continue to have a lesser impact on the city and the region than they do elsewhere.

Culture

Many non-Washingtonians have a hard time thinking of culture and Washington, DC, at the same time. The city is often assumed to be a cultural wasteland compared to other major American cities. A half century ago, this belief may have held a grain of truth. But no longer. In the last quarter century, the city has begun to realize George Washington's dream of a place of culture and learning.

If we use "culture" to mean performing arts, visual arts, and intellectual life, Washington has much to offer. It is a city of music, which is available in many different venues: several major concert halls, parks in the summer, churches, embassies, universities, museums, coffee houses, and pubs. In addition to an opera company, a ballet company, several major choral societies, a well-regarded symphony orchestra, and several chamber music ensembles, the city has as diverse an array of musical events as any city in the United States. Situated between the North and the South and with rural areas within an hour's drive, Washington offers a great mix of urban popular music and country and bluegrass music, together with a considerable amount of folk music. The city is also an important stop on the national jazz circuit. With a large African American community, Washington is a place of gospel singing and has even produced its own style of popular music known locally as go-go. And for those looking for free concerts, military bands play almost every evening in one or another public area in the summer (as well as at Constitution Hall in December). Free concerts are also held during the summer at Farragut Square, throughout the year in the National Gallery of Art, and on important national holidays such as the Fourth of July on the Mall and Memorial Day and Labor Day on the Capitol's grounds.

But what makes the cultural scene in Washington unusual is the variety of ethnic music—from South Indian to Latin American, from Celtic to Korean, and much more—available in the city and its environs. In contrast to many American cities with large immigrant populations, Washington draws a sizable portion of its foreign-born residents from Asia and Africa, as well as Latin America, and many of these groups have their own cultural societies and community organizations. Within these groups are highly educated individuals, who often work for the many universities and embassies, the World Bank, the Inter-American Development Bank, or the International Monetary Fund; businesspeople; and unskilled laborers. The mix of ethnicities and classes gives rise to a cosmopolitan music scene that brings in both highbrow (with frequent Indian sitar music) and popular performers—for example, well-known singers and musicians from Latin America and Africa.

The theater scene has also developed considerably over the past several decades with venues such as the Sidney Harman

Hall and the Folger Theater hosting visiting companies and several resident companies that offer classical drama (there is a Shakespeare company), modern drama, and edgier experimental plays. Dance—classical, ballet, and modern—is on offer but seemingly less dynamic than theater. The same goes for exhibitions of local artists. Painting, photography, and sculpture galleries have been expanding rapidly in the city with, one hopes, much more to come. The city, local businesses, and philanthropists provide essential support for all of these cultural activities, and the city has undoubtedly benefited from the expanding individual, private sector, and corporate giving that accompanies the monetary contributions.

If we extend our notion of exhibition art to those works on display in DC but not created here, the city must be considered one of the great art venues in the world with the diverse and valuable resident collections and visiting exhibitions in several major art galleries: the National Gallery of Art, the Smithsonian National Portrait Gallery and American Art Museum, and the Phillips Gallery. These galleries typically combine their exhibitions with periodic musical events: Sunday orchestral and chamber concerts; Friday evening jazz concerts at the National Gallery; Thursday and Sunday evening wine, music, and lectures at the Phillips. Indeed, the art aficionado in DC can have few complaints about the quality and quantity of art on show at any one time; there are probably more artistic events and exhibitions in DC per capita than in any other city in America. It is especially important to note that a large portion of art and cultural offerings in this city are free to the public. Such offerings are unparalleled in any other American city.

But one peculiar aspect about art in Washington is that almost all of it is created somewhere else and brought to the city. Put another way, the city consumes great art but seems not to produce it very often—at least not yet—with the one exception coming from the city's great African American musicians. Washington's otherwise broader artistic community has not produced a J. M. W. Turner to portray the city as he did for London; or a Fyodor Dostoyevsky, who situated his great novels in St. Petersburg and conveyed a feel for life there in the nineteenth century; or the poets' writing of St. Petersburg (Alexander Pushkin's "The Bronze Horseman") or of London (for example, T. S. Eliot's "The Waste Land"). While many talented artists and writers have called the city home, where is the high-quality body of painting, literature, or poetry *about* Washington?

Many have written works on the functioning and policies of the US government, and numerous society matrons have written about their lives in the city. Such works are often interesting, at times amusing, but not rising to literary masterpieces. Henry Adams, Henry James, Walt Whitman, and Mark Twain wrote about the city in the nineteenth century, but what they wrote was not part of their great works. Yes, the mystery novels of George Pelecanos and the political novels of Gore Vidal are set in the city and convey a sense of the place, but these books, while entertaining, are not great literature, either. Edward P. Jones's *Lost in the City*, a collection of short stories set in Washington, was a finalist for the National Book Award for Fiction, and his novel, *The Known World*, won the Pulitzer Prize. But the pickings remain slim.

Is there something about a primarily political city that is toxic to quality artistic creation? Perhaps the sacred (art) and the profane (politics) do not mix well. Active politicians often have little time or patience for the kind of reflection associated with great art, so a political city may be less appreciative of such work. If their concerns with power and policies and grappling with crises set the tone for a town, it may be a discouraging place for those artists who find politics a mundane inspiration for great writing. Politics, at least in contemporary America, also discourages eccentricities; indeed, if the media catches you being unconventional, you may not win reelection. Any ambiance that avoids eccentricity and reflection may discourage great art, which seems to thrive in a space to experiment. Also, the often-gritty nature of politics—focused as it is on power, ambition and pretention, conflict and compromise, favors and deal making—may not lend itself to great art or literature (though it clearly presents opportunities for excellent political humor). Especially in democracies, publicly supported art is subject to public judgments that may be conservative or not consistent with artistic quality or experimentation, and so discourage both. (A number of controversies have arisen over the years involving art supported by public monies, with objections to nudity, sexual topics, and other themes deemed offensive to public taste and morals.) So maybe political cities such as Washington, Brasilia, Canberra, Islamabad, and Ottawa are doomed to live with a fundamental inconsistency between great art and politics, at least until they break free of their primarily political orientation.

George Washington wanted his nation's capital to be a place of intellectual endeavor, with a great national university, scientific investigation, and societies for intellectual debate and exchange. He did not get his great national university. But the city does have many well-regarded private universities, one public university, and numerous colleges, institutes, and graduate schools within the city limits, plus several large universities in the suburbs of Virginia and Maryland. In fact, in 2013, university students made up 10 percent of the city's population. All of the educational institutions organize seminars, conferences, and performances on a daily basis during their academic terms, drawing on their own considerable expertise, on the competencies in official Washington, and on the skills of private analysts and officials and experts from other places. Anyone interested in politics and public policy sooner or later comes to Washington to speak and work.

In addition, the city is replete with think tanks such as the Brookings Institution, the Carnegie Endowment for International Peace, the Aspen Institute (where my son works), and many other venues for research and discussion on any and all varieties of public policy. One estimate has the number of think tanks at well over three hundred. Most of them hold frequent public discussions and lectures on topics of their concern. In addition to all these places of thought and discussion, in recent years many government institutions also have organized seminars and presentations, with the Smithsonian Institution (half public and half private) being perhaps the most prolific by hosting an astonishing array of events each month. And each week, various locales somewhere in the city—bookstores, universities, or think tanks—host numerous book launches or poetry readings.

Probably there is no other city in the world with greater opportunities for intellectual exchange than in Washington. It is truly the "city of conversation" that Henry James dubbed it more than a century ago. But it tends also to be a relentlessly pragmatic city, not one involving deep theoretical probing, literary criticism, or philosophy. It is a city centered on political conversation above all. No one who has an interest in politics and the wider world has any reason to feel intellectually bored in Washington.

CHAPTER

5

Three People Who Made the City

ITIES ARE SHAPED by many things: major events such as wars or the needs of commerce or trends in human settlement. Once in a while, cities are also shaped by individuals. This chapter presents brief biographical sketches of three men who had a major impact on the city of Washington. We have already met these people in previous chapters. Here we can get a deeper sense of who they were and what they achieved. All three stories are an astonishing mix of triumph and tragedy. Let us start with the man who designed the city.

Charles L'Enfant

The person who has had the greatest influence on the cityscape of Washington is surely Pierre Charles L'Enfant. Thomas Jefferson, James Madison, and Alexander Hamilton agreed that the capital of the new country should be located somewhere along the upper reaches of the Potomac River. George

Pierre Charles L'Enfant (1754–1825).
Historical Society of Washington, DC

Washington decided the exact place and gave his name to the city. But the person who designed the city was L'Enfant.

L'Enfant was born in France in 1754 and grew up in Paris. His father was an artist attached to the prestigious Royal Academy of Painting and Sculpture, where Pierre Charles eventually studied. But a quiet career as an artist in Paris was not for him. He was one of those young Frenchmen, inspired by the ideals of the American Revolution, who traveled across the Atlantic to volunteer with the Revolutionary Army. He was wounded in the siege of Savannah, captured by the British, and exchanged in a prisoner swap. He became a captain in the engineers, attached to Baron von Steuben's staff at Valley Forge. He reportedly amused his comrades with his pencil portraits of them, and later the general Marquis de Lafayette asked him to paint a portrait of General Washington. (He completed this portrait, but it has since been lost.) It was the first but not the last encounter that the young Frenchman would have with George Washington (who remembered him as "Langfang").

L'Enfant ended the war as a major and thereafter began to work on a variety of projects in New York City, including redesigning the city hall and designing coins, furniture, houses, and the medal for the Society of the Cincinnati, headed by George Washington, for those officers who had served in the Continental Army and Navy. In 1789 when it became clear that a new city would be created as the seat of the US government and that George Washington would decide its locale, L'Enfant wrote to the then president and offered his services to design the new capital "on such a scale as to leave room for that aggrandizement and embellishment which the increase of the wealth of the Nation will permit it to pursue at any period, however remote." The president, probably impressed with L'Enfant's expansive view of what a grand new capital would look like, agreed to give L'Enfant the commission and thus began the work that would produce the city of Washington today.

L'Enfant the Person

Before turning to the tortuous story of L'Enfant's work on designing the seat of government, let us consider what manner of person L'Enfant was. What would our impression of him be today if he were, say, a dinner partner?

L'Enfant was tall—around six feet—and erect, with a military bearing. Although there are no portraits of him, a sketch of his face and comments of those who met him suggest he was a handsome man who was clean shaven and pulled his thick, long, wavy hair to the back, as was the custom of the day. His face was nicely proportioned with a prominent nose.

He was described as polite and gentlemanly. He was also very proud and full of ideas with an expansive sense of grandeur. He was intense and sometimes imperious, and he could be obstinate and unyielding in his views. Not known for his political instincts or his tact, he was often heedless of reasonable constraints (including those involving money) on his decisions, but he was also generous with his own resources.

L'Enfant would likely have been an attentive dinner companion and an interesting conversationalist but passionate on topics of importance to him, such as his architectural projects. One imagines that he would have dominated the dinner conversation if the topic of designing the nation's capital arose, airing all the frustrations he suffered and brooking little disagreement with his opinions. He would not have been concerned with the cost of the dinner, whether he or someone else paid.

L'Enfant was apparently also a solitary man; he never married, and accounts of his life do not include references to any close companions. He was, however, deeply committed to George Washington. A workaholic, he seemingly cared little for the schmoozing that even at the beginning of the American Republic helped to lubricate human relationships and eased resistance to change. Finally, he reportedly exhibited an artist's absolute belief in the rightness of his aesthetic judgments. One suspects that having dinner now and then with L'Enfant could have been insightful and energizing. Frequent dinners, though, could well have proven exhausting at best and tedious at worst.

The City's Design

At President Washington's behest, L'Enfant proceeded immediately to Georgetown in early March 1791 to begin planning the new capital, which, it had been decided, would be a ten-mile square diamond that would include Georgetown, Alexandria, the confluence of the Potomac and Eastern Branch

(Anacostia) Rivers, and parts of Maryland and Virginia. The territory closest to the confluence of the two rivers would be the city of Washington; the rest would be the territory of the District of Columbia.

L'Enfant reached Georgetown on a rainy and foggy afternoon. He promptly paid his respects to the mayor and settled in at Suter's Tavern (since demolished). In the several days that followed, also rainy and foggy, L'Enfant rode and walked over much of the territory that was to be the new city. He found forests—what is today Capitol Hill was densely wooded—and old fields and orchards. Scattered houses and shacks sat on the properties of the major landowners. There were also plentiful streams, some overflowing with the continuous rain, producing marshy areas around the watercourses.

L'Enfant was delighted with what he found: a fan-shaped flat area, more or less triangular, that rose from the Potomac and Anacostia Rivers with a slightly elevated terrace running east–west through its center. Farther inland from this terrace were the hills that marked the beginning of the Piedmont Plateau. The area was intersected by several streams, including Tiber Creek, which rose north of Jenkins' Hill, flowed around its base, and emptied into the Potomac just above its confluence with the Anacostia. Rock Creek was the other major stream flowing through a valley that separated Georgetown from the area L'Enfant saw as the main part of the new city.

By the time President Washington turned up at the end of March, L'Enfant had developed his understanding of the terrain and his ideas enough to satisfy the president. Washington ordered him to continue working and have more detailed plans ready by the end of April. L'Enfant visited Mount Vernon at the end of June with his plans well elaborated. L'Enfant's plan was both grand . . . and expensive. But Washington liked it and rejected a much more modest plan for the capital city that Thomas Jefferson had sketched: a small grid of several streets that included a Capitol and a President's House, set relatively close to one another, with little aesthetic interest or charm and certainly no grandeur.

Washington now had to persuade the landowners of the properties located within the intended city to turn them over to the federal government and to find a way to finance the new city's construction given that the federal government had limited resources and other, more urgent priorities. As noted in chapter 2, he persuaded the landowners to deed their properties to the government, and later they would receive half of any undeveloped land back for sale to speculators and to people who wished to reside in the new capital. At the same time, the federal government would also sell some of the properties it had acquired (using the rest for public purposes) and use the receipts to finance the city's construction. To convince prospective buyers to risk their monies on lots in the proposed city, Washington needed copies of the design plan. But L'Enfant failed to deliver them in time for the first sale of lots.

L'Enfant later argued that the printer had not completed the plans in time. But the designer was also strongly opposed to the timing of the sale; it was too early, in his view. Further, he was also thought to be against the idea of financing the city's construction by selling property to private speculators.

He preferred that Congress appropriate the funds. Some thus suspect that L'Enfant was responsible for the maps not being available. But whatever the reasons, the absence of the maps likely contributed to the potential buyers' lukewarm response. Washington was disappointed, but he exonerated L'Enfant for this unfortunate incident.

The next problem involving L'Enfant was much more troubling. Daniel Carroll of Duddington, the owner of the largest local estate, had begun constructing a house that extended several feet into one of L'Enfant's planned boulevards. L'Enfant asked Carroll to remove the house. Carroll understood from one of L'Enfant's staff that removing the house would not be necessary, so he continued its construction and appealed for an injunction against its removal. Nevertheless, one day L'Enfant sent his workmen to demolish the house, and they promptly did. Carroll was incensed when he discovered his house was gone. Daniel Carroll's uncle, one of the three commissioners Washington had appointed to oversee the development of the city, and one other commissioner sent Washington an angry letter about the incident.

Other conflicts occurred that displeased the commissioners as well as Washington himself. Another landowner planned to build a house that would have extended into one of L'Enfant's streets, raising again the issue of who had the authority to prohibit such buildings. Next, although L'Enfant submitted to Washington a long list of costly supplies needed for the coming building season, he refused to submit his list to the commissioners for their consideration and approval. These clashes led two of the commissioners to threaten to resign rather than work (or try to work) with L'Enfant. Washington had remonstrated to L'Enfant to yield a little to the wishes of the landowners: "It will always be found sound policy to conciliate the good-will rather than provoke the enmity of any man, where it can be accomplished without much difficulty, inconvenience or loss." But Washington's counsel had no impact on the unyielding L'Enfant. Washington, running out of patience, wrote to Jefferson that "there is a line beyond which he [L'Enfant] will not be suffered to go. Whether it is zeal—An impetuous temper—or other motives that leads him into such blamable conduct, I will not take it upon me to decide."

When both Washington and Jefferson requested that L'Enfant acknowledge the authority that the commissioners had over the planning of the city and L'Enfant as its planner, the latter refused absolutely. Frustrated with L'Enfant's intransigence and deepening conflicts with the commissioners and landowners, Washington finally fired L'Enfant almost a year from the date he had hired him to design the new capital.

The rest of L'Enfant's story is a sad one. He refused the payment offered for his services in the planning of Washington, DC, apparently regarding it as so small as to be derisory. He resented the changes in his plan (though they were not major ones) made by his successor, Andrew Ellicott. However, having failed to copyright the plan he made, L'Enfant received no royalties from it in the future. He picked up a number of other design projects in other parts of the country, but his impulse to overdesign and his inability to get along with supervisors led to a string of failures. He finally returned to Washington, DC, and began to request payments for his previous work from Congress. He received and accepted two payments, which were immediately garnished by his creditors. He later turned down an appointment to teach military engineering at the United States Military Academy at West Point, averring that he did not think he would be a good teacher.

He spent his last years living in penury, haunting the halls of Congress for financial redress without effect. In 1815 he took up residence at Warburton Manor, the seat of Thomas Digges on the Potomac across from Mount Vernon, and for a time L'Enfant helped reconstruct a fort, now called Fort Washington. Finally after Digges died, his nephew William Dudley Digges invited L'Enfant to live with his family in Chillum, just east of the city limits, at his Green Hill estate. In a sweet historical irony, he was welcomed by William Digges's wife, the daughter of Daniel Carroll, whose house L'Enfant had torn down three decades earlier.

Pierre Charles L'Enfant died in June 1825 only weeks short of his seventy-ninth birthday. The value of all of his possessions at that time was a mere $45. He was buried under a tree on the Green Hill estate.

L'Enfant's Contribution to Washington, DC

As the city of Washington grew over the remainder of the nineteenth century, L'Enfant and his plan seemed forgotten. A number of changes took place that compromised the plan. For example, as noted previously, the Treasury Department was built across Pennsylvania Avenue, interrupting the grand vista from the Capitol to the White House. The west side of the White House was turned into government offices. The Smithsonian buildings impinged on the Mall, but in any case, it never became the site of the formal gardens that L'Enfant had foreseen. Perhaps the worst change was that the railroad ran tracks across the Mall to a train terminal located on the Mall itself.

By the last quarter of the nineteenth century, the city and the country had grown in size, in wealth, and in pride of its accomplishments. The centennial of Washington, DC, was also fast approaching. Citizens as well as political leaders, including then president James Garfield, began considering how to make the city into a world-class capital. They turned to L'Enfant's plan as a guide in their proposals to renew and beautify the city. At the turn of the century, the resulting McMillan Commission's plan was based very much on L'Enfant's ideas and concepts. The Mall was renewed and the trains and train station relocated. New memorials, including the Lincoln Memorial, were sited with a view to maintaining and extending L'Enfant's long vistas. One memorial, a tomb in Arlington National Cemetery overlooking the city, became L'Enfant's final resting place in 1909. He was honored in a grand ceremony, one he would have surely appreciated, for his contributions to the city and to his adopted country.

Washington, DC, today is, to an extraordinary extent, very much the city that L'Enfant planned more than 224 years ago despite the inevitable adjustments and changes in that plan. The beauty and force of his concepts have endured and have made Pierre Charles L'Enfant the most influential individual in establishing the shape and beauty of the capital of the United States of America today.

Alexander Robey "Boss" Shepherd

Alexander Shepherd was born in the city only ten years after L'Enfant died. Shepherd was destined to be second only to L'Enfant as the most important person who shaped the cityscape and the future of Washington, DC.

Shepherd's father was the owner of a prosperous lumber business. However, the death of his father forced Shepherd to drop out of school at age thirteen and work to support his mother and seven siblings. When he was seventeen, he became a plumber's apprentice in Washington's largest plumbing firm. Shepherd joined the militia at the beginning of the Civil War and served his three months' enlistment, after which he returned to work at the plumbing firm. After a few years of energy and hard work, he was promoted to a partner in the firm and later became its owner.

Shepherd then invested his increasing income into DC real estate, banking, transportation, and a host of other businesses in the city, thereby expanding his wealth. Meanwhile, he married and fathered seven surviving children. Shepherd also began joining civic associations and became active politically, as many Washingtonians have done after they gained success in their careers. In 1867 he became part owner of the *Evening Star*, giving him an outlet for his views on local pol-

ALEXANDER R. SHEPHERD

Alexander Robey "Boss" Shepherd (1835–1902).
William Tindall

itics of the day. This outlet gained prominence as the debate on the future location of Washington again emerged.

The Civil War had badly degraded the city's already poor infrastructure: unpaved streets covered by mud or dust, a lack of adequate sewerage or access to clean water, the pestilential Washington Canal running through the downtown area, and a host of other problems. Congress had no inclination to fund a major upgrade in the quality of the city's infrastructure, and the tax base of the city itself was still too limited to support such a costly enterprise. More and more proponents of moving the nation's capital elsewhere—perhaps to St. Louis, perhaps to Cincinnati—were speaking out. Something had to be done.

Another problem involved the complications of managing an expanding territory that was really three politically independent entities: the old city of Washington itself, Georgetown, and the "county" or District of Columbia, which covered the area beyond the original city boundaries set by L'Enfant. Coincidentally, in 1868 the city's charter, put into place at the beginning of the 1800s, was set to run out, thus opening an opportunity to rethink how the city should be organized and spurring considerable debate over several years on the topic. There was also the reality of an increasingly important black vote as suffrage was granted to Washington's growing number of African American male citizens in 1867. Many among Washington's white elite, a number of whom had earlier owned slaves and whose sympathies in the Civil War had been with the South, did not welcome this change.

Shepherd and a group of supporters began to agitate for a new charter that would combine the old city, Georgetown, and the county of Washington into a single political entity. The territory would relinquish its decades-old self-government, thereby effectively disenfranchising its black citizens, and replace it with officials appointed by the president. Congress passed legislation reflecting these proposals in 1870 and stipulated that the president would appoint the mayor and council and that citizens would elect a twenty-two-person legislature.

It was generally thought that President Grant would name Alexander Shepherd the first governor of Washington, DC, but the president chose to appoint the brother of one of his rich friends to the position. Shepherd instead became one of three public works commissioners. This decision would have major implications for the future of the city.

Shepherd the Person

Before continuing with the story of Alexander Shepherd, let's stop and try to picture what sort of person he was. Perhaps we should arrange a dinner with him as we did with L'Enfant.

Alexander, or "Boss" as he came to be known, was six feet tall and powerfully built. He was a clean-shaven, handsome man. His picture shows a calm and even gentle face but with a hint of determination in his eyes.

In photographs, Shepherd looks much like an American of today, in contrast to L'Enfant, whose manner of dress, early life of European aristocratic privilege, and birth in the eighteenth century seem to put him beyond the reach of familiarity in the twenty-first century. Shepherd reportedly had a deep, musical voice, was genial, and was given at times to unconstrained laughter. He was considerate to his friends and colleagues. He could read other people well and could be tactful and persuasive when necessary. Apparently he would have been a pleasant and engaging dinner companion. And he probably would have been an interesting conversationalist given his involvement in so many local enterprises and issues.

But these attractive qualities belied another side of Shepherd. He was a man of enormous energy and described as audacious, determined, cunning, and ruthless. He was given to outbursts of temper when frustrated in his goals, exhibiting a typical Type A, hard-charging personality in an age when such personalities rose to the top of the worlds of business and commerce. He was surely a pleasant dinner companion and could be a good friend but not someone to cross or impede.

Shepherd's Contribution to Washington, DC

At the first convening of the board of public works, Shepherd effectively took control. He had himself appointed vice president and thereafter tacitly ran the board. He appointed an advisory panel of distinguished individuals and solicited advice on what was necessary to upgrade the city's infrastructure and the probable cost. Even before he could officially award contracts for work on the streets, he approved the beginning of regrading downtown. He persuaded the territorial legislature to approve $4 million to pay for the improvements.

Shepherd's haste alarmed some in the capital who succeeded in getting a judge to impose an injunction against further work. Shepherd then stopped work in areas where his opposition was the greatest, leaving streets torn up, piles of bricks in inconvenient places, and other impediments to movement. He figured that their opposition would diminish when they needed him to complete his work so they could use their streets.

Shepherd's tactics to override obstacles to his work did not stop there. He decided to eliminate the Northern Liberty Market at what is now Mount Vernon Square. The market was noisy and dirty and competed with a larger market farther downtown in which Shepherd had a financial interest. The merchants had persuaded a local justice of the peace to issue an injunction against Shepherd's demolishing the market, but the night on which the injunction was expected, the justice was persuaded to have dinner out of the city. By the time he returned, Shepherd's workers had pulled down the market.

Soon after the Northern Liberty Market incident, Shepherd requested that the Baltimore and Ohio Railway remove its tracks from First Street, Southwest. The tracks, laid during the Civil War for military purposes, remained in place and were an obstacle to regrading the street. The company refused. Its men woke up one morning to find all of its tracks gone except for the few rails under one of its locomotives.

Shepherd's work proceeded at a whirlwind pace and included paving more than 150 miles of roads and sidewalks and installing nearly 125 miles of sewers plus gas mains, water mains, and street lights. He had more than 60,000 trees planted, many of which still survive. And he filled in the noxious Washington Canal, which now flows under Constitution Avenue. However, in his haste, he graded streets without regard to the situation of the houses bordering them, so some found their front doors well above grade and others several feet below grade. Homeowners were not amused. District residents were even less amused by the increased property taxes they had to pay to finance these breakneck improvements. Some, it was said, even had to sell their houses to pay the taxes.

What soon became clear was that Shepherd had paid little attention to the costs of his improvements. An audit demanded by the growing number of angry citizens showed that he had way overspent his funds. Congress imposed a ceiling on what Shepherd could borrow for his public works, but a later audit found that he had spent at least double that ceiling and probably a good deal more (if books had been kept adequately). In not a few cases, contracts were negotiated under questionable circumstances. No action was taken against Shepherd, though there was much grumbling about self-dealing and corruption.

In 1873 President Grant appointed Shepherd governor of Washington, DC. But it was a short-lived governorship. The city was effectively bankrupt, and the ensuing panic of 1873 further weakened the finances of the city and many of its residents. Congress investigated the finances of the board of public works and other elements of the local government. Finding extensive mismanagement and insolvency, it decided to abolish the territorial government and replace it with three commissioners, appointed by the president, to manage the city. Boss Shepherd's service to the District of Columbia was over.

Three years later, Shepherd declared bankruptcy himself and moved to Mexico to run a silver mine and rebuild his fortune. As he did so, he paid several subsequent visits to Washington, DC, but never returned permanently. He died in 1902 and was buried in Rock Creek Cemetery in the city that he had done so much to improve.

Looking back on Boss Shepherd's successful efforts to improve the infrastructure of Washington, it's not hard to assume—as he undoubtedly did—that as in the past, Congress would refuse to allot the money to make the desperately needed improvements. And he probably figured that whatever he spent and however he spent it, Congress would have to pay the debts he ran up anyway. He was clearly right. Now it's difficult to imagine how Washington would have become the city it is today without the boost he gave it at a crucial time in its history.

Marion Shepilov Barry

In 1979 Marion Barry became the second elected mayor of Washington, DC, under home rule and eventually served four terms as mayor. This first election and the mayor himself symbolized a historic shift in power of the city: It moved from the whites in Congress and the president's office to the poor and working-class blacks who made up the majority of the city's electorate. (Although the first elected mayor of DC, Walter Washington, was an African American, many regarded the former bureaucrat as having assimilated into the white establishment insofar as that assimilation was possible for blacks.) The word "symbolized" is important here since Barry won office with the overwhelming support of poor blacks along with that of liberal whites, the gay community, and elements of the white business community in his first terms. He placed a number of his close political supporters from the civil rights movement in positions of power and implemented policies aimed at promoting black empowerment. He also enacted policies to benefit white business interests seeking to abolish or curtail rent control.

Barry's third and fourth terms were marked by a deterioration in public services in the city, deepening fiscal woes,

Marion Shepilov Barry (1936–2014).
Courtesy DC Public Library, Star Collection/Washington Post

problems of corruption, and his own arrest and imprisonment (between the third and fourth terms) for cocaine use.

The extent to which his four terms as mayor actually benefited his black constituents is still being debated, but it is
certainly clear that many of them, especially in the poor sections of the city, continue to see him as an advocate who was
committed to their interests and well-being and was not
afraid to confront the white establishment openly—and often
in racially charged terms. When Marion Barry died on November 23, 2014, he was still a hero to many in the city but a vil-
lain to many others.

Marion Barry was born in Mississippi in 1936, one of ten
children. His father died when he was four, and his mother
moved the family to Memphis, Tennessee. Barry had a number of part-time jobs as a youngster to help with the family's
finances. He then won a scholarship to study at LeMoyne
College in Memphis, Tennessee. He earned a master's degree
in organic chemistry at Fisk College in 1960 and began a
PhD in chemistry, first at the University of Kansas and then
transferring to the University of Tennessee–Knoxville. In
1964, as the civil rights movement gathered momentum, he
dropped his studies and moved to DC in 1965 to become the
leader of the city's Student Nonviolent Coordinating Committee. He proceeded to get involved in a number of political
activities, including protests in favor of home rule, boycotts
of bus fare increases, and efforts to raise awareness of municipal hiring practices and police brutality. He also helped create Pride, Inc., funded by the federal government, to provide
job training and other opportunities for unemployed black

youngsters. Inspired by Great Society goals and in the midst of national political changes associated with expanding civil rights for blacks, the federal government was grappling with what to do about the country's young blacks and feared that their limited educations and future job prospects would lead to street protests and violence.

Barry soon became well known about town as a militant supporter of black ambitions and a source of funding for jobs and job training. In 1971 he decided to run for a position on the board of education and gained a seat in 1972. (As one of the few elective positions in DC, a position on the board was an obvious step for aspiring politicians. Unfortunately, it also led to a politicization of the school board.) In 1974 Barry ran for and won an at-large seat on the DC Council. Adding to his luster, he survived being shot by Hanafi Muslims in 1977 during a siege of the District Building. Finally in 1979 he became DC's second mayor.

Barry is credited with helping to rejuvenate the downtown areas of the city, spurring the new construction that eventually brought the area back from the riots. He created a summer jobs program for all Washington youths and promoted minority contracting for DC government purchases, thus channeling resources to black businesses and community organizations in the city. In the early years of his tenure as mayor, he balanced the city's budget and enabled the city to enter the bond market with the highest credit rating available.

Barry's second term was marked by ballooning expenditures by the DC government, deteriorating services, rising crime rates, and embarrassing scandals involving several of his colleagues in the DC government, stories about his channeling city contracts to supporters and cronies, and speculations about his womanizing and use of drugs. Barry's third term, beginning in 1987, was marked by his declining performance as mayor and increasing rumors that he was using crack cocaine. Once the drug appeared in the city, crime and especially homicide rates escalated. Washington soon became known as the murder capital of the U.S. In a sting operation in 1990, the FBI arrested Barry for using cocaine in the hotel room of a former girlfriend—and caught the whole affair on videotape. He was convicted for possession and sent to jail for six months.

Barry emerged from prison and ran for mayor once again in 1994, and once again, he won. This term was marked by such serious problems with the city's huge deficit and other debt that Congress moved control of the city's finances out of the mayor's hands and into a newly created financial control board. Later, control of most key decisions on finances, hiring and firing, and other issues were also put under the control board. In effect, home rule had been temporarily suspended.

When his term was over in 1999, Barry did not run for reelection as mayor. But in 2004, he ran for the District Council seat representing Ward 8 and won. Despite continuing brushes with the law over unpaid taxes, traffic infractions, and other problems, the former mayor served on the council until his death.

Barry the Person

Marion Barry was a tall, dark man with a receding hairline. When he was younger, he often sported a mustache. In his early days in Washington, he was slim and walked with an easy but energetic gait. His voice was deep, and he had a distinct Southern accent. Films show his charm, but he could also be confrontational and threatening.

Barry's long career reflected his ambition, audacity, and resourcefulness. He knew how to position himself as the indispensable interlocutor and negotiator between the white establishment and the black community—in particular, the angry and potentially violent black youths. He was an astute politician who was able to put together unlikely coalitions of white liberals (and the *Washington Post*, which endorsed all of his mayoral elections), black youths, unions, and eventually business interests to support him. Through all of his successes and travails, he maintained the support of poor and working-class blacks.

He was also cunning: one minute acting as a militant street dude and, in another, as a moderate and reasonable collaborator with the establishment; one moment provocative, contrite the next. He could sound ideological, railing against capitalism, and in other circumstances, he could be opportunistic and solicitous of business support. Barry called himself determined, and many have echoed that judgment. His long history of ups and downs and ups again in local politics more than justifies that accolade.

As a dinner partner, one imagines him as charming, engaging, and full of fascinating insights and stories of politics in Washington, DC. But his failures as mayor—and those failures are legendary—cast a long shadow on his successes. So what justifies his inclusion in a short list of individuals who have had a major influence on the evolution of the city?

Barry's Contribution to Washington, DC

Marion Barry's achievements or failures are not what make him an important figure in the pantheon of Washington's leaders. His relevance lies in what his multiple elections as mayor symbolized—an opening to political participation and power of not only the traditional elites of the black community in Washington but also of the many working-class and poor African Americans in the city.

Washington, DC, has always had a robust African American community. Yet for much of the city's history, economic conditions, public services, and civil and political rights for this population have been circumscribed or eliminated. With the election of Marion Barry, the poorer segments of the black population finally felt they had someone relatable in power to represent their interests. He spoke for them and was seen as one of them, despite his misbehavior and clashes with the law. Indeed, many of his conflicts and especially the FBI's sting operation against him that resulted in his imprisonment for cocaine possession were seen as simply another effort by the white establishment to suppress black people's ambitions and rights. Affronted African American members of juries failed to convict Barry of many of the indictments against him, and often judges and prosecutors ended up dropping charges. Ultimately the voters remembered his civic roles. They saw Marion Barry as representing the hopes and aspirations of working and middle-class African Americans seeking political power and equality.

Barry's experiences fit a basic narrative that many in the black community embraced: For hundreds of years the white establishment tried to oppress them, but as Barry's life so powerfully illustrated, they had the determination to rise again and carry on. One young African American man in a 2013 television newscast about Barry observed that he served as a role model for any "black man in this city that has fell [*sic*] down but was scared to get up and brush the dust off. . . . People are saying, 'If he can do it, I can do it.'"

There may be more to the story behind Marion Barry's history in DC. When a long-marginalized or excluded group finally gains power, the people often express an exuberance that is little constrained by the tedious demands of responsible governing. They have a hunger for change, a deep distrust of the old leadership, and a tolerance of behavior on the part of their new leaders that under normal times the people might criticize and sanction. This pattern is evident in postcolonial African countries immediately after winning their independence and among the populist regimes in Latin America that enjoy the support of indigenous groups or working classes. Indeed, it is a frequent product of opening up a political process to all people. It may take many years to pass, but with each new generation of citizens gaining a greater ability to engage in the political process and the economy, it often does happen.

That evolution seems to have occurred in Washington, DC. The kind of broad and unquestioning support Marion Barry enjoyed in the past greatly diminished with time. More technocratic politicians, intent on improving services in the city and managing its finances more effectively, have won the last four mayoral elections. In a historic sense, Marion Barry marked the turning of a corner in Washington politics, and that development argues for his inclusion as one of the small handful of the most influential people in the history of the city.

CHAPTER
6

Washingtonians

A s OF 2014, there were 658,893 Washingtonians. So who are they? First of all, the notion that there is no such thing as a "Washingtonian" because of the overwhelmingly transient nature of the city is a myth. The Census Bureau tells us that nearly 80 percent of the city's population in 2014 lived in the same house they had inhabited the year before. Given that this percentage is the same as the national average, why do so many believe that Washington is a city of transients?

Surely the answer is because the members of the political class—presidents, members of Congress, political appointees, diplomats, and their staffs—*are* often transient. Many come to the city to serve in political positions and leave when their terms are completed. (Well, actually many do not leave. They take lucrative positions as lobbyists, consultants, lawyers, or experts at think tanks and hope for appointments in the next administration.) But the political class in Washington is not large, despite its attention from the media. First, there are only 535 members of Congress. Next, as identified in the *United States Government Policy and Supporting Positions* (*Plum Book*), an annual listing published by either the House or the Senate (they alternate) to identify presidentially appointed positions, approximately seven thousand "leadership and support positions" exist in Congress and the executive branch. If you assume an average of ten employees rotate in and out of each of the two hundred embassies in Washington, then there are another two thousand migrants. Thus, assuming all of these positions are filled by out-of-towners (but they are not), probably ten thousand people are potential transients. Nevertheless, these changes make the news, and their stories are most likely the source of the myth that DC is a city of transients.

But to be fair, the notion that born-and-bred Washingtonians, especially of more than one generation, are scarce has some validity. I am a third-generation Washingtonian, and my son is a fourth, but finding others with such long ties to the city is rare. While some Washington families, working class and professional, are longtime residents in the city, much of the professional class comes to the city from elsewhere to study or work and then stay. When they have their children, many families move to the suburbs to take advantage of good public schools. Once their children are grown, the empty nesters often return to live in the city. This churning of population gives an additional sense of transience to Washington.

So we return to our question, who are Washingtonians?

Race and Ethnicity

Race and ethnicity are ever-present elements in the story of Washington, so let us start there. Washington is a majority-black city, but demographic changes are occurring rapidly. As of 2014, 48 percent of the population was African American, 36 percent was white, and the remainder identified as Hispanic or Asian. Washington's black population hit a peak of 71 percent in 1970 and has been dropping since. The white population, peaking at 75 percent in 1920 but declining thereafter, began to climb again in 2000. The Hispanic population was only 3 percent of the city in 1980, but since then its percentage of the total population has been rising rapidly.

Within the foreign-born population, 44 percent come from Latin America, with the largest number from El Salvador. Asian immigrants, or 18 percent of the foreign-born population, are divided between Chinese, South Asians, and Vietnamese. Europeans and Africans make up another 19 percent and 16 percent, respectively. These immigrants are diverse in terms of class as well. Some of the highly educated work at international organizations or embassies; others work as professionals—for example, doctors and researchers. Those who come from abroad to work in international organizations often become permanent residents, while foreign embassy employees, who usually leave after their two- or three-year assignments, are considered visiting residents. Some immigrants find work in construction, drive the ubiquitous DC taxi cabs, or operate many of the city's corner grocery stores and dry cleaners. The large immigrant communities that have settled in the suburbs outside of the city also contribute to the cosmopolitan culture of the metropolitan region.

Looking forward, if current trends continue, by 2020 Washington's long history as a majority-black city may change, although blacks will remain a plurality for some time to come. African Americans will by then be approaching 45 percent of the population, while whites will be around 40 percent. Hispanics will likely reach 10 percent or more, and Asians may exceed 5 percent. The components of recent population changes show the percentage of black residents in the city dropping roughly a percentage point per year as middle-class and poor blacks move to the southern and eastern suburbs outside Washington. White professionals (mainly unmarried individuals or families without children) are meanwhile returning to the city. And the large inflow of immigrants to the Washington metropolitan area, including the city of Washington, that has made it a major "immigration gateway" is a trend that seems set to continue.

One additional demographic factoid: Washington, DC—at a little more than 4 percent in 2002, according to the US Census—has the highest percentage of same-sex couples of any state in the nation. This data only compares "states" but includes the District of Columbia; it did not include data for cities. Another 2013 study estimates that a little more than 10 percent of the population of DC identifies as gay, lesbian, bisexual, or transgender, including couples and singles.

Where do all these groups live in Washington? Washington is still very much a segregated city—not by law, of course, but by circumstances: perhaps subtle but continuing discrimination, differences in the economic resources available to buy or rent houses, and in some cases, preferences of individuals. For a long time, affluent whites have lived west of Rock Creek Park in Georgetown, Cleveland Park, and points north, where housing is most expensive. After redevelopment in the 1960s, Southwest became a predominantly white, middle-class neighborhood. Historically although not uniformly, wealthy, middle-class, and poor blacks have lived east of Sixteenth Street in the northeast and southeast parts of the city and their adjoining suburbs.

There has also been a degree of segregation by choice regarding entertainment in Washington. Depending on their location and the type of activity involved, churches, major theaters, many restaurants, and other entertainment venues, except professional sports events, often attract predominantly either white or black audiences. The famous statement that "the most segregated hour of Christian America is eleven o'clock on Sunday morning," attributed to Dr. King, is less true today than it was fifty years ago, but voluntary segregation still exists in many of Washington's churches. However, conversations with young black and white professionals suggest that now they share more of their culture, entertainment, and friendship than ever in the past. Perhaps there is some hope for the postracial era that is much talked about in the media and is surely advanced by the election of the first black president in 2008.

Poverty

Race is not the only dividing line in Washington. Class is important too. And here the differences are quite stark. Washington has more wealth and more poverty than the US national average, and that disparity is reflected in education as well. Nearly 36 percent of Washington's families have incomes higher than $100,000 per year, while only 23 percent of families nationwide averaged that much in 2009. Nearly 18 percent of Washington families live below the poverty level compared with 15.5 percent nationwide. The figures for education are even more striking: Thirty-one percent of Washingtonians older than twenty-five years of age have a graduate degree compared to only 11 percent nationwide, but 10 percent of Washingtonians—or 3 percent lower than the national average—never graduated from high school. Predictably, high levels of wealth and education are concentrated in the white community, while poverty is concentrated in the black community. Let us note, however, importantly, that three-quarters of Washington's African Americans are from the middle or working class.

The sources of poverty in Washington are familiar ones: being poor in the first place, coming from a single-parent family, suffering from health problems (sometimes including alcohol, drugs, and mental health challenges), having little access to services, attending some of the least effective schools in the nation and earning a limited education, finding few job prospects or training, and often living in insecure and crime-ridden housing projects. The pattern of those trapped in the poverty cycle is a common one in many American cities: dropping out of school, having babies at a young age, getting into trouble with the law, and then finding it difficult to obtain even low-paying jobs. Poverty thus gets passed on from generation to generation.

Poverty is not new in Washington, DC. Indeed, it was the plight of many African Americans from the South who fled to the city during the Civil War and in the late nineteenth and early twentieth centuries to escape harsh racial treatment. Arriving with few skills, these immigrants were segregated into the decrepit alleys and slums, and many of their children lived similar lives. Nevertheless, others were also able to escape poverty over the generations through education, hard work, and good luck. Looking into the future, the decreasing number of jobs, the low pay for unskilled workers, and the ability to escape poverty for those with a limited education seem likely to worsen, especially as the premium on higher education rises in the job market. How to help the poor escape from their various poverty traps is perhaps the greatest social challenge facing the city of Washington today.

Social Washington

Washington, like all cities, boasts a social elite. Indeed, for much of its history, it had *two* social elites that existed apart—one white, one black. Conventional "society" in Washington is still predominantly white, though prominent African Americans are increasingly joining that world, and that change appears to have accelerated with the election of a black president.

Who are the members of Washington's "proper" society? Those with prominent positions, often but not always related to politics; those with elite family connections; those with money; and, of these groups, those who want to be part of society—meaning, they are willing to devote their time and resources to socializing. Their names are probably in *The Social List of Washington, D.C.*—also known as the *Green Book* due to its emerald cover—which has been published annually since 1930. (One has to be nominated by someone already in the *Green Book* to be included in it.) Some of them are on a notional "A List" of usually thirty or forty individuals who are exceptionally socially visible and in demand.

Politics is at the core of Washington society, and the president and First Lady can set the tone for that society if they wish. In fact, a social invitation from the president is regarded as a command; it cannot be turned down except for health reasons. Among the most sociable presidential hosts were the Kennedys. With their taste for dazzling social occasions at the White House, they gave a boost to the city's social life in what had been for many years a pretty dull town. Their dinners remain the standard by which presidential entertaining is still judged and often found wanting.

In contrast, President George W. Bush had little interest in Washington social life, leading some to complain that "society is dead" during the Bush years. President Obama is not much more involved in the Washington social scene either and sticks to obligatory entertaining for heads of state or cultural icons. One magazine that tracks Washington's social life has complained that "the President and First Lady haven't exactly been emulating the Kennedys and Reagans on the Washington social scene, preferring discreet dinners with Valerie Jarrett and other Chicago pals and the occasional foray to Ben's Chili Bowl or Ray's Hell Burger with the likes of Nicolas Sarkozy and Dimitri Medvedev."

Individuals close to the president (even informal advisers outside of government), cabinet officers, senior members of Congress, Supreme Court justices, and ambassadors from prominent countries typically have automatic entrée to Washington society if they want it, though not all do. Prominent hostesses often compete for their presence at their dinners.

The political nature of Washington makes its society life different from that in all other city's societies in the United States. When politicians lose elections, resign, get fired from cabinet posts, or depart when their president's term is over, their position in society often ends. They may remain part of Washington "society" on the basis of their past prominence, but they need to fortify that position on the basis of their wealth, ongoing activities, or other sources of prominence. Indeed, a large portion of Washington society can disappear in a period of a few weeks, only to be replaced with newcomers when a new president and Congress are elected. As a result, Washington society has been more fluid and open to newcomers than those societies in many American cities where long-established families (for example, the Boston Brahmins or the New York Knickerbockers) have been effectively able to exclude new money or the socially ambitious.

During the late nineteenth century, that very openness is what drew the newly rich to Washington to build their mansions and entertain lavishly. One observer complained that "Lucifer himself will be welcomed if he will dress well, keep his hoofs hidden in patent leathers, and his tail out of sight."

Although Washington society has had a fluid membership, its rules of behavior have been some of the most rigid—thanks again to politics. Protocol, based on a formal list of precedence established by the White House, governs where people sit at dinner and, at very formal occasions, who escorts whom to what table and in what order. Protocol can also determine who sits where in a car or in someone's office, who stands or sits where during ceremonial occasions, and who leaves an airplane first in an official delegation.

From the beginning of the American Republic, an elaborate code of etiquette involving "social calling" was never formally published but known to Washington society and strictly enforced. This practice involved the wives of newly arrived public figures or private families wishing to join society. The new arrivals would call on those wives whose husbands held higher ranks than their husbands or whose acquaintance they wished to make. The newcomers would either appear in person on designated days, giving the butler their personal card, or send their own footman to deliver their card on their behalf. If they called in person, they turned down the upper right-hand corner of their card to signal they were present. (It was very important to turn down the appropriate corner of their card. Should they accidentally turn down the lower right-hand corner, it would signal they were sending condolences for a death or other family tragedy—a grave and probably fatal social mistake.) If the person on whom they were calling wished to receive them, they would be invited in for what was supposed to be a rather formal chat of between fifteen and thirty minutes. After the call, the hostess could acknowledge the call by paying one herself on her caller (at best, within three days), and thereafter, she could issue an invitation for dinner, tea, or other event if she wished to open a relationship. Wives had regular reception days when they were "at home" to receive callers. Those days could depend on their husband's official position: cabinet wives one day, Senate wives another, wives of Supreme Court justices a third, and so on.

The elaborate and pretentious etiquette of social calling (not to mention the political corruption of Washington, DC) prompted Mark Twain and Charles Dudley Warner to write an amusing spoof of it in their book, *The Gilded Age*, published in 1873. Social calling, however, extended well into the twentieth century. It finally ended during the Second World War when gasoline and food rationing (and the growing number of people on whom calls had to be made) made the practice simply too difficult to sustain.

The custom of social calling was a weeding-out process to determine who was acceptable in Washington society as well as a way to help integrate new arrivals into that society. Today Washington women in society do not make formal calls; instead, informal arrangements serve to introduce the spouses of prominent officials to one another and to society.

For example, several private "international clubs" meet periodically for lunch. Made up of a selection of spouses of Senators, cabinet members, diplomats, and others, the clubs' leading prominent socialites invite the newcomers to become members. Other informal but exclusive clubs serve similar purposes of bringing established members of society together and integrating new members. Their memberships are all by invitation only as well.

Finally, politics in Washington affects society in yet another way: It can make social occasions important nurturing and networking opportunities. As in most of the world, politics is lubricated by personal relationships that create trust and ease the process of getting things done. Dinners organized by prominent members of society bring political figures together so they can get to know one another, exchange information, and make deals in a private, informal setting. Indeed, during much of the latter half of the twentieth century, prominent hostesses—almost all of whom lived in Georgetown and included Pearl Mesta, Pamela Harriman, Evangeline Bruce, and Katharine Graham—played an important role in Washington politics for just those reasons. By 2010 the prominent hostesses of an earlier age were gone, and similar social leaders have not replaced them. Cocktail parties (other than those for fund-raising purposes) and three-martini lunches have diminished as well in an increasingly workaholic Washington. Further, women who might have been hostesses in the past are choosing now to be busy professionals. These changes not only make for a more serious and sober city but also have prevented the development of the kind of friendships across party and organizational lines that once facilitated politics. The harshly partisan tone of Washington in recent years may have been one of the consequences of these changes.

Another segment of Washington society is called "cave dwellers." Typically members of long-established, wealthy, and prominent families, they have a secure place in society but tend to stay out of public view. The term "cave dwellers" was first used in the nineteenth century to refer to Washington's original families—the large landowners who sold their properties to the federal government for the construction of the capital city—along with other wealthy families who came to live in the city. They were mostly Southerners, usually with a strong sense of propriety and refinement, who withdrew from active social lives after the Civil War when an influx of brash, often-uncouth Yankees took over the government.

Washington society is open now to those with money as well as those with political or family connections. And perhaps more than at any other time since the late nineteenth century, families with a great deal of money from private sources make up a visible part of Washington society. But it takes more than money to be welcomed into society in the nation's capital today. It is an expectation that those with money will give generously to local charitable or cultural organizations. (One of the local society magazines, *Washington Life*, publishes an annual list of wealthy individuals and families in Washington and how much they contribute to charity.)

Social Washington.
Mandel NGAN/AFP/Getty Images

Philanthropy opens doors to service on boards of important organizations, and service on such boards can open social doors in turn. Such boards might include those of the Kennedy Center and Children's National Medical Center, as well as boards of prominent museums, universities, and social service organizations. Even government agencies providing public services—for example, the National Archives—create their own foundations with boards of prominent Washingtonians for fund-raising purposes.

There are a variety of ways of joining Washington society. But what does it take to get kicked out of it? The answers I have received when I have asked this question are diverse. Some say one should not be boring; otherwise, there will be no invitations to dinners where lively conversation is expected. (Unfortunately, there are many dinners where no such conversation is likely.) One should not be drunk at public occasions. One should dress conservatively and not engage in eccentric behavior. One should not offend public morals; no corruption or sexual scandals that make the news, please. Anticipating such problems at the beginning of his administration, President Jimmy Carter reportedly ordered two of his staffers to marry the women with whom they had been living. Offenses involving children are fatal to membership in society. But many of these strictures (except the last one) are relaxed for the most senior political figures and persons of power and prominence, and many transgressions are known and tolerated as long as they do not become public.

White society in Washington no longer excludes people based on their race or religion. (Jews were also excluded from many private clubs until the latter part of the twentieth century.) While the number of African Americans circulating in Washington's elite society is still small, more are on the social "A list" of the most sought-after guests as they populate the senior ranks of the Obama administration. As noted previously, during the era of segregation in Washington, blacks created their own elite clubs and organizations and their own society world, with debutante balls, summer camps, and other rites of passage familiar in white society.

Traditionally, black society itself was stratified according to skin tone. Skin tone in color did not provide automatic admission to this society, however; other things counted too: family background, education, and affluence. Private clubs and other organizations that elite blacks might be invited to join include Jack and Jill, a nationwide social and cultural organization for mothers and children; Boulé, a national organization for black men; and Links, another national organization for black women; as well as particular fraternities and sororities. Reportedly, being accepted in black elite society in Washington is helped if one has ties to Howard University, the premier black university in America, and one's family has lived in Washington over several generations with an unblemished reputation.

Washington society today sees less formality and more tolerance and diversity, among both blacks and whites, in the increasing social relationships of the two communities. But with the growing demands of the workplace, where public officials, members of Congress and their staffs, lobbyists, lawyers, and diplomats now work much longer hours than in decades past, the city is focused more on work and less on being sociable. The convivial Southern elites and slow-moving bureaucrats of bygone eras must be turning over in their graves as many of today's DC professionals spend ten to twelve hours per day in the office and, when they do attend evening social events, stand around, squinting into their mobile devices or peeking at them under the dinner tables, and depart by ten o'clock so they can be ready for an early start the next morning.

What Are Washingtonians Doing Right Now?

Let us imagine it is a typical Sunday. How do Washingtonians usually spend the day? The answer is in much the same way as other Americans, with the possible difference that the hard-core political class scrutinizes the *New York Times* and *Washington Post* (or *Washington Times* if you are more conservative) and watches successive political talk shows on TV in the morning for policy signals and political gossip—particularly in an election year. They might read their newspapers on a mobile device. Those from the northeastern United States, especially New York, might eat a bagel and lox while reading the newspapers. Approaching noon, they might go to brunches at private homes (for the better off and better connected) or at restaurants (especially for young, in-town professionals).

But many Washingtonians are not well-off, well-connected, or hard-core political types. They may worship on the weekend. You can tell where the churches with large congregations are by the double- and triple-parked cars in front of and nearby the buildings. Sixteenth Street, which runs from the White House due north to the border of the city, is full of churches, synagogues, Buddhist temples, and other places of worship. In particular, this street should be avoided on Sunday mornings unless one is attending services there. The large, active black churches in town draw congregations from the city and suburbs, and there are large white churches, including a few evangelical megachurches, in and around the city. Individual churches also serve congregations that are made up of Africans, of Latin Americans, of Koreans, and of many other ethnicities as well.

After church many will watch sports games on TV. It is almost required that all Washingtonians watch Redskins football games, even during losing seasons, since conversations the next day at work will inevitably be about the Sunday game (and again after the Monday night or even Thursday night game). Others may work in their gardens, weather permitting, or do home projects or go shopping or visit friends or family. Recreation enthusiasts might break out their bicycles and head off along one of the many trails in the city. Others will spend some time at their local gym or health club and get on the treadmill to work off the past week's calories, while some will buy fresh produce at Sunday farmers' markets in town. Some Washingtonians will relax at their second homes on the Eastern Shore of the Chesapeake Bay or in the mountains of Virginia. Yet others may sleep in if they were in their offices most of their waking hours during the previous six days (yes, often working a half day on Saturday in the office is de rigueur for the busiest professionals) or if they spent most of Saturday taking their kids to play sports (soccer has become more and more popular), to take music lessons, or to engage in other self-improvement activities. The fifty thousand university students in the city, meanwhile, having returned to their dorms around daybreak from their parties, will wake up sometime in the afternoon and perhaps go to a local bar to help recover. Maybe they will break open their books once the sun goes down.

This Sunday schedule will sound familiar to Americans from all over the country. Washingtonians are really not so different—except that what is on many of their minds is politics and policy, and what awaits many of them in the coming week are long hours in the office and in myriads of meetings, as well as breakfasts, lunches, receptions, and dinners, that also relate to politics and work.

Turning to the yearlong cycle of life, when visitors come to Washington, they frequently use the words "handsome" and "quiet" to describe their first impressions of the city. These judgments seem fair. The city's monumental core is certainly handsome. And apart from a handful of thriving nightspots, its streets are very nearly empty of activity from more or less eleven o'clock in the evening until eight in the morning. The city is really quiet during August and around Thanksgiving and Christmas when people leave the town for the holidays.

But the seeming calm of the city can be misleading. The city is very busy during the workweek though the sense of that energy, which is so evident in dense, high-rise places like New York, is dissipated somewhat by the openness of Washington. And then, while some might take in one of the cultural events in the city after work, many will go on to attend social events that help them network or, for the young, meet other Washingtonians.

The annual cycle of life in the city is partially shaped by the political calendar. Congress opens its legislative session on January 3, shortly before the president gives the State of the Union speech. Thereafter begins the busiest period in the city, with breaks of only a few long weekends, until Memorial Day at the end of May. Memorial Day marks the start of summer, but there are typically two more months of intense work before Congress recesses and the city empties in August. As in Europe, in Washington it is simply not possible to get anything done in August since most people flee to the seashore or the countryside or somewhere far away and cooler. Meanwhile, the city is crowded with tourists, especially along the Mall, from April to September.

After Labor Day, Washingtonians reoccupy the city as schools open and work begins, and the atmosphere remains intense until Thanksgiving in November. A little more energy is expended during the first two weeks in December, and then the town dissolves into Christmas parties and holiday preparations. The city finally shuts down a week before Christmas until several days after New Year's, when it gets going again. This cycle has much to do with the congressional schedule, which tends to set the tone for activity in Washington.

The rhythm of life in Washington is set by the political clock. But the real story of Washington and Washingtonians is that it has begun to change and become more than a political city. Its private sector is growing; its cultural offerings and neighborhood amenities are expanding. Further, its population is diversifying with the growing number of immigrants who bring their culture and cuisine with them, and the influx of young people drawn to the Obama administration has had an impact. After more than two hundred years, Washington, DC, is becoming the lively capital that George Washington and Pierre L'Enfant had envisioned at the beginning of the American Republic.

CHAPTER

7

Toward the City's Future

WHERE DOES WASHINGTON, DC, go from here? The history of the city's development, thus far, has been one of gradual progress toward realizing the dreams of its founders but with many detours and unexpected twists and turns. With that admonition in mind, let us imagine Washington in the year 2025, assuming past trends hold.

The increase in relatively affluent individuals and families will further spur the revitalization of the city, including many of the poorer areas of Northeast and Southeast. As it has in the past, gentrification, the other side of revitalization, will boost housing prices and press poor and working-class families to move to the suburbs. Public monies for low-income housing could modify these market pressures, but they will not be halted. And gentrification will not solve the problems of poverty. Instead, they will be shifted to another place and probably present one more difficulty for the poor as they try to commute to work. The homeless will not disappear, either; they will still populate downtown parks and beg on street corners.

As a result of these demographic changes, the proportion of the city's population that is black will fall—an evident trend that has already been mentioned—and the proportion of white and Hispanic citizens will rise. (One caveat: The impact of gentrification is also forcing many of the poorer and middle-class Hispanics out of the city, and that movement could lead to a smaller proportion of Hispanics in the city by 2025.) Washington may no longer be "Chocolate City," as many have called it; but even if they are not the majority, African Americans will continue to make up the largest proportion of the population. These changes will also alter the nature of politics in Washington, opening the way for more political competition and ethnic and racial alliance shifting within the city. A larger middle class will also demand better government and city services—another apparent trend—and the populist episode that made Marion Barry mayor for several terms despite the dismal performance of his administrations will be part of the past.

A more populous and affluent population will hopefully lead the city to introduce even better amenities: more entertainment, restaurants, in-town shops, and, hopefully, an even larger and better art scene. If the budding commercial sector of the city continues to grow and to contribute to the art scene, as well as to demand more exhibition and performance arts, then Washington could enjoy a truly diverse cultural environment with greater variety in livelihoods and lifestyles. Maybe even a Washington school of painting or literature could develop.

What will lifestyles be like for Washington professionals in 2025? What will race relations be like by then? How will Washingtonians entertain themselves, and will they continue to be workaholics, as many are today? The answers ride in part on the evolving values and visions of today's younger generation. In the mid 2010s, I confess I have too little a sense of the world of twenty-year-olds with their social media, mobile devices, Facebook posts, and tweets. I have the impression that for those twenty-five years old and younger, not only has technology made it possible to work longer hours, including outside the office, through emails and texting and files in the cloud, but these same devices are also at the center of a dense, networked social world in cyberspace. I wonder what it all means for traditional face-to-face human relationships. What, for example, is really going on with the couples strolling hand in hand down Connecticut Avenue, with each person using his or her cell phone?

My millennial son suggests that another change in Washington taking place in his generation involves race but not class. "For my generation of middle-class professionals, born in the 1980s and later, the walls between whites and blacks in the city are no longer there," he says. "We work together, attend the same clubs and parties, enjoy many of the same musical performances and, of course, sports events. However, walls between the poor and everyone else are still as strong as before."

The possible future of Washington in 2025 is a hopeful one, at least for those able to afford to live in the city. The city seems to have entered a virtuous circle in which its quality of life improves and attracts more affluent residents, ones who demand a yet better, more comfortable, and vibrant city. This situation contrasts sharply with the vicious circle of the 1950s and 1960s when white and black flight abandoned the city to poverty and crime, and those problems, in turn, encouraged more Washingtonians to flee to the suburbs. Regarding Washington's future, however, possible problems could block or reverse my rosy scenario, and there are some downsides to the future.

One regrettable result of an increasingly affluent city would be a decrease in the ethnic and class diversity that has enriched the area, especially in recent years. This diversity would not be entirely lost, but it would have to be sought mainly in the suburbs. The city would be poorer in an important way by this loss.

More menacingly, life in the city could be disrupted or destroyed after a major terrorist attack on Washington—which will remain an important focus for terrorists—depending on the means used. A dirty bomb or a chemical or biological attack could make parts of the city unlivable. Even a limited action could cause residents to move outside the (presumably) downtown target area or out of the city altogether. The increasing number of security structures being erected in the area, meanwhile, could also limit access to public facilities and ultimately damage the grace of the city itself.

An outbreak of a devastating infectious disease—for example, the long-anticipated bird flu virus—could not only reduce Washington's population (and the population of other urban centers worldwide) but also encourage people to relocate in the more open suburban areas. A major crime epidemic that is fueled, for example, by a new and cheap illegal drug (like crack cocaine in the past) could scare existing city residents and reverse the population growth.

A major economic depression could slow down significantly the trends described earlier and expand the number of those in poverty, though such a depression is likely to have less of an impact in Washington than in places with smaller government expenditures. A major racial incident could set off riots similar to those in 1968, though the poverty and anger in Washington's close-in areas of that time appear to be considerably less today.

One development seems likely by 2025: Global warming will make Washington hotter in the summer, warmer in the winter, and more insect ridden all year. (Mosquitoes in the summer are already exceptionally numerous and aggressive.) The warmer winters might be welcome and might prove to be an attraction for those people who now flee to Florida to escape the winter cold. However, it is hard to think kindly of hotter and more humid summers. Global warming could cause the Potomac and Anacostia Rivers to rise as well, increasing the likelihood of flooding in low-lying areas, such as south of the White House.

All of these dangers are possible, but there is reason to hope that the city and its citizens, inside and outside government, could find solutions. Washington, DC, has come a long way since its founding more than two hundred years ago in the forests and fields of the Potomac River valley. It has pulled through numerous near-death experiences and many other challenges and depredations as the city took shape. Almost miraculously, the original plan for the city has endured more or less intact. Washington, DC, seems set to continue to grow and prosper, becoming—even more than it already is—the grand and lively capital that George Washington imagined in the great democracy that he did so much to create.

Acknowledgments

C AROL LOVED THIS BOOK. It represented something deeply personal to her as she applied her analytical mind and the power of her words to understanding and explaining Washington, DC, a city she loved. When she became sick, she worked as much as she could on this manuscript, but she was unable to complete it before she passed away. It was only through the effort of some special people that we were finally able to publish her last contribution. Those people are Gail Griffith, Maurice Jackson, Gael Gahagan, Clare Ogden, Curtis Farrar, Richard Brown, and the staff of Georgetown University Press.

An additional thanks must go to those people who stood by us when Carol got sick and still stand by us today—in particular, the strong women of Georgetown University and beyond.

Notes

1
Why Washington, DC?

1   "great cities, like great men": Frederick Douglass, *In the Words of Frederick Douglass: Quotations from Liberty's Champion*, ed. John R. McKivigan and Heather L. Kaufman (Indianapolis: Indiana University–Purdue University, 2012), 62.

6   "that aimless stroller": Edmund White, *The Flaneur: A Stroll through the Paradoxes of Paris* (New York: Bloomsbury Publishing, 2001), 16, 40.

2
The History and Politics

16   "fed . . . with many sweet rivers": Francis D. Lethbridge, "The Architecture of Washington, D.C., 1791–1965," in *AIA Guide to the Architecture of Washington, D.C.*, 5th ed., ed. G. Martin Moeller Jr. (Baltimore MD: Johns Hopkins University Press for the Washington Chapter of the American Institute of Architects, 2012), 2.

17   "noble and cheerful": Andrew White, SJ, "Narrative of a Voyage to Maryland, 1633–34, translated from the Latin," Historic St. Mary's City Museum of History and Archaeology, 10–11, https://www.hsmcdigshistory.org/pdf/Voyage-Narrative.pdf.

23 "where the youth from all parts": Cited from Albert Castel, "The Founding Fathers and the Vision of a National University," *History of Education Quarterly* 4, no. 4 (December 1964): 285.

29 "a new country": Abigail Adams, "An Overnight Stay," Washington DC, 1800, EyeWitnesstoHistory.com/pfcapital.htm.

30 "This embryo capital": Letter, "To Thomas Hume, Esq., M.D., from the City of Washington." in Thomas Moore, *The Poetical Works of Thomas Moore* (New York: D. Appleton, 1868), 178.

34 "City of Magnificent Intentions": Charles Dickens, *American Notes* (Sandy UT: Quiet Vision Publishing, 2003), 90.

34 "the appearance of the metropolis": Fanny Trollope, *Domestic Manners of the Americans* (1832; Mineola NY: Dover Publications, 2013), 130, 131.

39 "I wander about a good deal": Walt Whitman, "Memoranda of the War: The White House by Moonlight, February 24," *Selections from the Prose and Poetry of Walt Whitman*, ed. Oscar Lovell Triggs (Boston: Small, Maynard, 1898), 24.

44 "an air of comfort, of leisure": Cited from Kathryn Jacob, *Capital Elites: High Society in Washington, D.C., after the Civil War* (Washington DC: Smithsonian Institution Press, 1995), 147.

52 "tangle of high speed roads": National Capital Planning Commission, US Commission of Fine Arts, "National Capital Framework Plan," July 10, 2008, draft, 20.

62 Census data on older American cities: US Census Bureau, compiled by Infoplease.com, 2005.

63 the most walkable of major American cities: See Christopher Leinberger, "Footloose and Fancy Free: A Field Survey of Walkable Urban Places in the Top 30 US Metropolitan Areas"

(Washington DC: Brookings Institution, December 2007), http://www.brookings.edu/~/media/Files/rc/papers /2007/1128_walkableurbanism_leinberg/1128_walkableur banism_leinberger.pdf.

3
Natural Washington

79   "an attractive basin": William Bushong, *Historic Resource Study: Rock Creek Park—District of Columbia* (Washington DC: US Department of the Interior, National Park Service, 1990), 24.

4
Cityscape

110   seventh largest population: US Census Bureau, "Population Change in Metropolitan and Micropolitan Statistical Areas, 1990–2003" (Washington DC: US Department of Commerce, Economics and Statistics Administration, September 2005), 9, table 6, https://www.census.gov/prod/2005pubs/ p25-1134.pdf; and US Census Bureau, "Four Texas Metro Areas Collectively Add More Than 400,000 People in the Last Year, Census Bureau Reports," press release CB16–43, March 24, 2016, http://www.census.gov/newsroom/press -releases/2016/cb16-43.html.

111   population of entire metropolitan area: Office of the Vice President for Planning and Institutional Effectiveness, Montgomery College, "DC-VA-MD-WV Metropolitan Area Demographic Data," 2016, https://cms.montgomerycollege.edu/EDU /Department.aspx?id=45952.

113   walk to work: US Census, "Modes Less Traveled—Bicycling and Walking to Work in the United States: 2008–2012"

(Washington DC: US Department of Commerce, Economics and Statistics Administration, May 2014), 8, table 1, https://www.census.gov/prod/2014pubs/acs-25.pdf.

114 "progressively larger, more sterile": Francis D. Lethbridge, introduction, in *AIA Guide to the Architecture of Washington, D.C.*, 4th ed., ed. G. Martin Moeller Jr. (Baltimore MD: Johns Hopkins University Press for the Washington Chapter of the American Institute of Architects, 2006), 3:13.

114 "elephantine aesthetic banality": Ada Louise Huxtable, *On Architecture: Collected Reflections on a Century of Change* (New York: Walker, 2008), 75.

115 "feudal twins": Christopher Weeks, *AIA Guide to the Architecture of Washington*, 3rd ed. (Baltimore MD: Johns Hopkins University Press for the Washington Chapter of the American Institute of Architects, 1994), 54, 57.

115 "big enough for two emperors": John Whitcomb and Claire Whitcomb, *Real Life at the White House: Two Hundred Years of Daily Life at America's Most Famous Residence* (New York: Routledge, 2002), 15. Clinton's quote is on page 468.

116 "architectural infant asylum": Richard D. White Jr., *Roosevelt the Reformer: Theodore Roosevelt as Civil Service Commissioner, 1889–1895* (Tuscaloosa: University of Alabama Press, 2003), chap. 1.

117 "But I don't want it torn down": John DeFerrari, "The Eisenhower Executive Office Building, America's 'Greatest Monstrosity,'" *Streets of Washington: Stories and Images of Historic Washington*, September 29, 2014, http://www.streetsofwashington.com/2014/09/the-eisenhower-executive-office.html.

117 "glorified candy box": Huxtable, *On Architecture*, 75.

127 Fortune 1000 companies: Caitlin Dempsey, "List of Fortune 1000 Companies by Urban Area," Geolounge.com,

August 14, 2014, https://www.geolounge.com/list-fortune
-1000-companies-urban-area/.

133   university students made up 10 percent: See "Percent of State
Populations Enrolled in College (as of 2013)," withmydegree.
org, https://withmydegree.org/higher-ed-enrollment-changes
-state/.

5

Three People Who Made the City

135   The greatest influence: This discussion of L'Enfant draws on
Saul Padover, ed., *Thomas Jefferson and the National Capi-*
tal (Washington DC: US Government Printing Office, 1946);
Paul Caemmerer, *The Life of Pierre Charles L'Enfant* (Wash-
ington DC: National Republic, 1950); Elizabeth Kite, *L'En-*
fant and Washington, 1791–1792 (Baltimore MD: Johns
Hopkins University Press, 1929); and Scott Berg, *Grand*
Avenues: The Story of the French Visionary Who Designed
Washington, D.C. (New York: Pantheon Books, 2007).

137   pencil portraits: Jed Graham, "Architect of a Capital Idea,"
July 21, 2006, http://www.arlingtoncemetery.net/l-enfant
.htm.

138   "on such a scale": Berg, *Grand Avenues*, 69.

143   "it will always be found": Caemmerer, *Pierre Charles L'En-*
fant, 181.

143   "there is a line beyond": Kite, *L'Enfant and Washington*, 75.

146   Evening Star: John DeFerrari, "The Evening Star Building,
Home to a Great Afternoon Newspaper," *Streets of Wash-*
ington: Stories and Images of Historic Washington, D.C.,
November 8, 2011, http://www.streetsofwashington.com
/2011/11/evening-star-building-home-to-great.html.

146   Alexander Shepherd was born: This discussion of Shepherd
draws on William Tindall, "A Sketch of Alexander Robey

Shepherd," in *Records of the Columbia Historical Society* (Washington DC: Historical Society of Washington, DC, 1911), 14:49–66; William M. Maury, "Alexander R. Shepherd and the Board of Public Works," *Records of the Columbia Historical Society* (Washington DC: Historical Society of Washington, DC, 1971–72), 71/72:394–410; and David Lewis, *District of Columbia: A Bicentennial History* (New York: W. W. Norton, 1976).

160 "fell down but was scared to get up": Fox 45 TV News, *Late Edition*, August 19, 2013, 11:03 p.m., https://archive.org /details/WBFF_20130820_030000_FOX_45_Late_Edition ?q=brush+the+dust+off#start/183/end/243.

6
Washingtonians

163 lived in same house: "Quick Facts: District of Columbia," United States Census Bureau, https://www.census.gov/quick facts/table/PST045215/11.

165 demographic changes: "Washington, DC," *Census Reporter*, 2014, http://censusreporter.org/profiles/16000US1150000 -washington-dc/.

165 foreign-born population: Ibid.; and "DC Latino Population by Country of Origin," Mayor's Office on Latino Affairs, http:// ola.dc.gov/page/dc-latino-population-country-origin.

167 additional demographic factoid: Daphne Lofquist, "Same-Sex Couple Households," *American Community Survey Briefs* (Washington DC: US Census Bureau, September 2011), https://www.census.gov/prod/2011pubs/acsbr10-03.pdf.

167 2013 study estimates: Gary J. Gates and Frank Newport, "LGBT Percentage Highest in D.C., Lowest in North Dakota," Gallup, February 15, 2013, http://www.gallup.com

/poll/160517/lgbt-percentage-highest-lowest-north-dakota
.aspx

168 income, poverty, and education figures: "Washington, DC," *Census Reporter*; and "United States," *Census Reporter*, 2014, http://censusreporter.org/profiles/01000US-united-states/.

171 Their dinners remain the standard: Maureen Orth, "When Washington Was Fun," *Vanity Fair,* November 5, 2007, http://www.vanityfair.com/news/2007/12/socialDC200712.

171 "the President and First Lady": "WL Lists: 100 Most Invited 2010," *Washington Life,* September 8, 2010, http://www.washingtonlife.com/2010/09/08/wl-lists-100-most-invited-2010/.

172 "Lucifer himself": Frank Carpenter, *Carp's Washington* (New York: McGraw-Hill, 1960), as cited in Francine Curro Cary, ed., *Washington Odyssey: A Multicultural History of the Nation's Capital* (Washington DC: Smithsonian Books, 1996), 82.

Index

Page numbers in italics signify graphics.

downtown, 3, 54, 60, 98–99
Dupont Circle, 102–4, 122

Early, Jubal, 38
Eastern Market, 102
East Wing, 120
Eden Center, 111
Eisenhower Executive Office
Building, 116–17
Eliot, T. S., 131
Ellicott, Andrew, 26, 143
Ellington, Duke, 46
embassies, 103, 124
Embassy Row, 102–3
eminent domain, 71
employment, 48–49, 126, 127
ethnic politics, 74–75

"facadomy," 122
Fall Line, 79–80, 140
Farragut Square, 129
federal government: and DC governance, 16, 41–42, 64–67, 70,
152; employment by, 49, 126;
land sales to, 38, 141; U.S.
Congress, 7, 65–66, 69–70,
149; as Washington's economic
engine, 126–27
FedEx Field, 60
Fenty, Adrian, 74
flowers, 88
Folger Shakespeare Library, 101
Folger Theater, 129–30
forests: in early Washington, 29,
140; of Rock Creek Park, 44,
77, 91, 92
freeways, 7, 51–53, 69, 98; and
"freeway fundamentalism,"
50–51
French embassy, 124
funding, 35, 71; under Boss Shepherd, 150, 152; congressional

subsidy, 69; for construction of
Washington, 27–28, 141–42; of
redevelopment, 61

Garfield, James, 145
gay community, 62, 104, 166
Gay Men's Chorus, 57–58
Gehry, Frank, 125
gentrification, 7, 63, 127, 185
geological zones, 79–80
Georgetown, 78, 167; DC incorpo-
ration of, 26, 66; establishment
of, 20, 80; neighborhood, char-
acteristics of, 104, 105–6, 122
Georgetown University, x, 11, 89,
106
German embassy, 124
The Gilded Age (Twain and
Warner), 173
global warming, 189
Graham, Katharine, 174
Grant, Ulysses S., 41, 152
Green Book (The Social List of
Washington, D.C.), 170
gun control, 69

Hamilton, Alexander, 22, 135
Harriman, Pamela, 174
Hispanics, 74–75, 165, 166, 186
historic preservation movement,
71, 121–22
homeless people, 7, 185
home rule, 7, 54–55, 66, 73–74,
157
Hooker, Joe, 37–38
Hoover, Herbert, 116
Howard University, 45–46
Huxtable, Ada Louise, 114

immigrants, 35, 74–75, 111, 129,
165–66
Inner Loop expressway, 51, 52